JACK MCMAHON

Atrophy and Asymptotes

A Father's Ravings on the Decay of American Values and Authoritarian Drift

First published by Recreated Dingo Books 2025

Copyright © 2025 by Jack McMahon

All rights reserved. No part of this publication may be reproduced, stored or transmitted in any form or by any means, electronic, mechanical, photocopying, recording, scanning, or otherwise without written permission from the publisher. It is illegal to copy this book, post it to a website, or distribute it by any other means without permission.

First edition

ISBN: 979-8-9997507-0-9

This book was professionally typeset on Reedsy. Find out more at reedsy.com

Contents

Preface		iv
1	Gun Control	1
2	Abortion	17
3	Drug Legalization	30
4	Deviancy	39
5	Free Speech	41
6	Reparations and Affirmative Action	50
7	Coronavirus Lockdowns	64
8	Voting and Democracy	88
9	Foreign Election Interference	98
10	Ideological Signaling and Fiduciary Duties	104
11	Social Security	112
12	Federal Reserve and Monopolies	119
13	Violence as Backbone of Society	127
14	Heroes and Demons	136
15	On Sources	144
16	On Prejudice and Morality	147
17	On Logic	153
18	On Death – The Final Asymptote	156

Preface

To my daughter,

In my own life, I grew up in a whirlwind of emotion and drama from an early age and it never really seemed to have an end point. It must have ended at some point, but there was no announcement to begin the peace time or declaration of victory or surrender in the wars I created with everyone around me along the way. The result of this was that time just kind of passed without me realizing that diplomacy and discussion were once again on the table between myself and the people I cared about.

There were points along the way that I realized I had not delved into deep discussion with many of my family and friends, save a few. I definitely expressed my opinions on the issues of our time, but never got many thoughts reciprocated. These were topics from anything concerning politics, culture, morality, responsibility or anything more than surface level "how're you doing?" conversations.

I don't know if this was due to strained relationships, guarded personalities or just indifference on issues that I believed to be of the utmost importance in life. It also could have been because I was raised in a broken home with many children. It is possible that there was just no time left in the day for my parents to have a personal relationship with each of their kids after splitting custody and work. It seemed to me that we, the children, essentially had to raise ourselves and each other. Any lesson we learned was from each other's mistakes and our own. Any bonds we formed were brought on by experiencing shared struggles. There was no time to sit down and be taught a lesson.

I do not want that for you. I am writing this now while our relationship is good and you are young because I know situations can change suddenly. It may not always be the case that you feel you can talk with me about anything. It may not always be the case that we can have our deep conversations about life on long car rides like we do now. I know myself and I know that I can be hard to talk to, but that shouldn't mean that you are forced to go through life somehow not really knowing your dad that you see everyday.

The following are issues that I feel are important to our time. I hope that I can explain my opinions on these issues to give you an understanding of why I think and act the way I do. I do not expect you to have the same opinions as me throughout your life. Every parent hopes that their child is BETTER than they are, but this will help you to understand who I am. It will help you understand some of the opinions and topics that you will encounter in your life and hopefully help you to think critically about each of these issues before forming your own opinion on them.

I love you and trust you will remain an amazing person,

Dad

(Note from Legal: The entirety of this book can be assumed to have the word "Allegedly" in front of it)

1

Gun Control

Let's begin with the highest law of the land: The constitution. What does it have to say about our rights on the matter of weaponry?

"A well regulated Militia, being necessary to the security of a free State, the right of the people to keep and bear Arms, shall not be infringed."

OK. I guess the argument is over.

Or so any logical person would think. Yet here we are, more than 200 years later, still hearing arguments about why we should infringe this right. The arguments you will hear will usually be emotional reactions to tragedies that occur in the country or systemic problems with violence. They will include pleas to reduce gun violence, prevent mass shootings, prevent mentally unstable people from having weapons, protect women and children from abusive husbands and fathers, protect police officers that in turn protect us, or ensure that we can shop, walk or do any daily activity without the constant dread of being shot.

Unfortunately for those making these arguments, none of them override the dangers that the second amendment was meant to protect against. That's right. An armed population is the protection, not the danger. The constitution was made to protect the citizens of this new country from existential threats. The number one existential threat to citizens throughout the entirety of history has been government. There have been countless government caused deaths since 2000 BC. That isn't very fair to guns, though. They weren't even alive, yet. Yes, we must anthropomorphize guns when dealing with those that argue for gun control. They believe they are sentient, willful, having intent and the ability to act. Let's just count the deaths caused by governments since "fire lances" were invented in the 10th century. An exact count will always be speculative, but we will be dealing with numbers so different by comparison of government caused deaths vs private gun deaths that finding the exact counts will be unnecessary.

We have wars that were forced upon the populations. From medieval times up to more "modern" times of the writing of the constitution and continuing on to the truly modern times, governments have been massacring their own citizens and the citizens of other countries by the millions. A lot of different countries, each with a lot of different wars is going to add up quickly. Just a quick glance for now: World War 2 had an estimated 70 to 85 million government caused deaths. OK, but sometimes one side doesn't put up much of a fight. Enter genocides and purges. Just to name more recent ones: Armenian genocide adding 1.5 million deaths, the Holocaust adding 11-17 million deaths, Stalin adding 20 million deaths, Mao adding 40-70 million deaths, Khmer Rouge adding 1.7 million deaths and the Rwandan Genocide adding just under 1 million deaths. Side note: If I forgot someone's favorite pet genocide to mention, it's clearly because I wanted to dehumanize you specifically, not because I'm just a random guy writing a book rather than a genocide researcher. (These are the sarcastic disclaimers we must make in today's world.) *Sigh*

Wow, that's a lot of death caused by government. Well, governments not only use warfare to kill. They also use lawfare to kill. The policies they put into place via just the THREAT of violence also kill. Enter

Starvation. Let's do a quick "just the last century" run down. Chinese famine: 15-45 million. Soviet Famine: 3-7 million. Bengal Famine: 2-3 million.

Finally, let's add in the biggest genocide denial in human history. 50-60 million abortions worldwide every year since the 20th century with a total in the billions.

So we've got a few categories of government caused deaths running at once. Wars in the 100s of millions. Genocides potentially up to another 100 million. Famine and starvation potentially up to over another 100 million and abortion in the billions. Depending on if you want to count abortion we could say it is either half a billion or multiple billion.

The estimated gun deaths throughout history, excluding government caused deaths, is estimated to be in the tens of millions. This number is including homicides, suicides and accidents. When it comes to suicides, having a gun or not having a gun is not going to be a determining factor for a suicidal person. Anyone that truly wants to end their life will end their life. Aside from that, it is a victimless "crime." The only person injured intended to injure themselves. As for accidents, I would beg any rational person not to consider these numbers, as well. Doing so would require the rational mind to investigate accidental deaths in thousands of other categories that no one is ever going to give up from driving automobiles to eating string cheese. Accidents and violence are two completely different subjects and no one is claiming that ladders are violent because people fall off of them. True gun violence in situations that have both a non-government perpetrator and a victim number in the millions throughout all of history, as opposed to the tens of millions number mentioned previously. Let's use 5 million since these are estimates and we don't know whether it is 2 or 9 million.

Five million vs FIVE HUNDRED million. (Using the conservative number that does not include abortion) Governments have been 100 times as dangerous as an armed population since the inception of guns and I even shaved off a bunch of government-caused deaths because the lists were too long and I'm just proving a point, not building a statistical database.

As shown, the data proves we need protection from governments more than we need protection from each other. With this data backing me up, I now feel comfortable putting it simply in an anecdotal example. If you are being mugged by someone with a gun as their weapon, you could potentially fight back and win. (especially if you have a gun!) If you are being mugged by someone with a government as their weapon, what chance do you stand? There is only one chance of surviving and it is 300 million people behind you, all equipped with their own guns. It is because of this that the second amendment is not simply the right to own a weapon, it is the right to use those weapons for your own protection against forces that would unjustly restrict your freedoms.

Some may argue that it isn't an armed population keeping the evil forces of the world at bay. "American politicians are just above the human nature that has shown its face time and time again throughout history." Sure, Jan.

OK, for the sake of argument let's not ASSUME that our government is just like the governments throughout all of human history. Maybe we lucked out and hit an evolutionary breakthrough that has destroyed the human need for control in those that wish to obtain power. Or rather than assume, we should look to see if they are performing actions often seen before government atrocities. Is our government looking to disarm the population? If not, why are we having this conversation as a society? Some of them clearly are. Is disarmament of the population a marker for upcoming atrocity?

The Ottoman Empire began disarmament in 1915. Between then and 1917 the Armenian Genocide takes place killing 1.5 million people. Joseph Stalin in the Soviet Union began disarmament in the 1920s. The Great Purge occurred in the 1930s. Nazi Germany disarmed demographics in

1938, followed by the Holocaust in the early 1940s. Mao Zedong enacted gun controls after the Chinese Civil War, followed by both the Great Leap Forward and the Cultural Revolution. The Khmer Rouge disarmed citizens after gaining power in 1975. In the following four years Pol Pot killed close to 2 million people.

This is just the societal marker leading up to genocide and atrocities for this topic. Let's check if any of these other markers describe our society. Dehumanization and derogatory language: We see that on both sides. I'm guilty of it myself. Go search "subhuman" or related words on Twitter. (It's not "X" until Elon Musk makes good on his promise of free speech absolutism, but that's another chapter.) Polarization along ethnic, religious or political lines. I would have said America had moved past ethnic and religious polarization when I was growing up, but a refusal to move into the future together from entities that benefit from polarization has given them a resurgence. Surely, no one can argue that political polarization is not present in American society. Laws and policies discriminating against demographics are clearly seen in affirmative action and similar policies.

Systematic denial of civil rights is seen in abortion law. (If you are pro-life, the baby's rights. if you are pro-choice, the mother's) Access to education and employment are both being denied on the basis of skin color every day for the majority of citizens. Establishment of propaganda networks and media has long been established at least since Operation Mockingbird and gets ever more obvious each day. The Smith-Mundt Modernization Act of 2012 reinforced this. Political instability is always occurring in the United States, as protesting is one of our most treasured rights. These often turn to riots. We definitely have a history of discrimination, along with every society that ever existed, so we have deep seated resentment always present as a potential marker. Targeting of demographics by leaders has been seen in the persecution of Christians and traditional families via the IRS, FBI and DOJ in general.

Showing up to school board meetings to prevent pedophiles from accessing your children has been deemed domestic terror by extremists in charge of the justice system. Silencing of dissent and whistleblowers from the COVID-19 exaggeration of 2020 made it the American norm for the government to collude with big tech companies and social media platforms to quelch even questioning of the state sponsored propaganda.

The biggest common marker I see in America is the indifference of a large percentage of the population. The ends are ever polarizing, stretching the common core values further and further apart, while the middle 80% of the population is frozen in either cowardice or nihilism. This was one of the very reasons I had stated for writing this book. I do not want you to ever not know what I believe. I would consider that one of my biggest failures. I respect the 10% on the opposite end of the polarization more than I respect the 80% that stands for nothing. That weak 80% will always give credibility to any government wishing to commit atrocities via their lack of action.

The markers are there in our government and our society. Anyone that wishes to disarm you should be treated the same as someone that wishes to commit atrocities upon you. The proper response of that society is to not only ensure your right to HAVE arms, but to actually USE them before it is too late. Good God, it feels great to write that knowing my Google Docs account isn't going to get banned, like it would on any public forum. GO, BOOKS!

Let's take a moment to think about the type of person that commits these acts against their citizenry and other peoples. What action do you think they would deem beneath them? If killing by the millions can fit into your moral framework, would assassination of one person also fit in? I think it would. Would the killing of children? I think it would. Surely, some of those millions were children. If they are willing to commit genocide, they are willing to do almost anything. I probably don't need the "almost" there. The type of people that disarm a nation are the type of people that want no resistance for the acts they are about to perpetrate.

History tells us what those acts will likely be. A willingness to perform those acts implies that anything and everything can fit into their moral framework and that any conceivable means is justified by their end in their mind. They are not above assassinating dissenters. They are not above killing children. They are not above propagandizing their population. They are not above taking away your God given rights as a human being. To them, you are not human. You are a piece in a game to be played with to win. If you add all of these observations together, looking at national tragedies becomes much scarier than they appear to be. Keep these things in mind when a radicalized 10% with some backing from an indifferent 80% create an emotional outrage in an attempt to take any of your rights, specifically your second amendment right.

Am I suggesting some national tragedies could be intentionally created as a tool for oppression? Well, I just said *keep them in mind* when you see a national tragedy followed by a call for rights restrictions. Let's look at history to see why. To be fair and critical of myself, the fact that these are considered false flag propaganda campaigns might ITSELF be a propaganda campaign. If that is the case, it would still prove my point that false flags, propaganda and state sponsored lies exist.

The year: 1933. The location: Berlin, Germany. The Reichstag building: currently on fire. Adolf Hitler uses this false flag to blame a Dutch communist to follow up with a suspension of civil liberties and prosecution/persecution of political opponents. Comparing this event to America, we have the prosecution of a political opponent in full swing today (2024) with Peter Nvarro, Steve Bannon and Donald Trump playing the part of Marinus van der Lubbe, the Dutch communist and the Biden Administration and DOJ playing the part of Voldemort. Errr, Hitler.

1939, The Gleiwitz Incident. Nazis disguised as Polish soldiers stage an attack on a German radio station as an excuse for military invasions. This one did not directly have a civil rights forfeiture for German citizens, but didn't end up too well for Polish citizens.

WAIT A MINUTE! These are "literal nazis." (to be spoken in Purple Hair voice) This is AMERICA! We would never...

1964, The Gulf of Tonkin Incident. Attacks on US Naval vessels in the Gulf of Tonkin were later discovered to be exaggerated. Potentially, 1 of 2 officially stated attacks never even happened. The result? Lyndon B Johnson gets America fuckin' PUMPED UP about killing some Vietnamese.

1962, Operation Northwoods. The Joint Chiefs of Staff and United States Department of Defense draw up false flag plans to allow American intervention in Cuba. John F Kennedy rejects the proposition. (Good Job, bro. I hope it worked out for you.)

1967, USS Liberty. Israeli Air Force and Navy attack the USS Liberty. The state sponsored story is that it was a case of mistaken identity. Guess we need less countries with Red, White and Blue flags. Pretty big "whoopsie, my bad."

OK, so the United States has shown that it can and has planned, performed and participated in false flags, propaganda and state sponsored lies. Here are a few more from around the world.

1954, Lavon Affair. Bombings in Egypt with US and British targets performed by Israeli intelligence to frame Egyptian nationalists. Operation Gladio, pretty much the same thing but it was NATO blaming left wing groups. The controversial 1999 Chechen Apartment Bombings in which it is suggested that the Russian Federal Security Service bombed apartment buildings in Russia and blamed Chechens as an excuse to escalate war.

Should we say "False Flag!" every time someone dies of unnatural causes? Of course not, but they do happen and it is likely that we didn't catch them every time they did it. So we know that they happen, but it will always be hard to tell when. A good way to find potential cases would be to look at tragedies that precede restrictions of freedom. They are used as an excuse to do morally questionable actions, and the ones we care about are the ones that affect us.

The Civil War led to Abraham Lincoln suspending the writ of habeas corpus and implementation of martial law. First Amendment rights were stripped even from Northern press or anyone that questioned government actions. No trials necessary. I'm not going to sit here and say I wish the South won because I do believe that slavery is evil. I'm also not going to sit here and say that Abraham Lincoln was a champion of freedom when he took away basic human rights from his citizenry. No specific examples of false flags come to mind in the Civil War, but that's not to say there weren't any and that's not to say his assassination wasn't warranted due to his stripping away of his peoples' right to free speech, whether or not that had anything to do with the assassin's actual intent and self rationalization for doing so.

World War 1 led to the Espionage Act and the Sedition Act, which further restricted freedom of speech and freedom of the press. If these acts were only used to protect American troops and military movements, it would be one thing, but in reality they are used to strike fear into those that would expose government wrongdoings.

The Great Depression ushered in the Emergency Banking Act and the National Industrial Recovery Act. The first allows the government to interfere with banks in the name of financial system stabilization. The second, while it lasted, gave the president industrial and labor regulatory powers that were eventually found to be unconstitutional.

World War 2 brought about concentration camps for 120,000 Japanese Americans and the War Powers Act. The president was granted powers to influence and control resources and production for purposes of war efforts.

The Cold War led to an old school cancel-culture of anyone suspected of being a communist or associating with communists. I'm obviously not a big fan of communists, but using their idiocy as a tool to steal freedoms is just as bad.

Social unrest during the Civil Rights Movement led to the FBI surveilling civil rights activists and using information gathered to discredit any actors that were not pro-government.

Attacks on the Twin Towers and other targets nationwide on September 11, 2001 furthered those surveillance programs with the Patriot Act to watch communications, finances and personal records. The Department of Homeland Security came shortly after, which just ended up being a tax on our time and cost to travel. Guantanamo Bay was used essentially for habeas corpus suspension again, along with state sponsored torture programs. Following the 9/11 attacks, a state sponsored lie was put out about weapons of mass destruction in the Middle East. Together, the attack and the lie led us into going to war with an entire region because they... "Hate. Our. Freedom." What a crock of shit. We don't even have freedom and even if we did, that is the most illogical reason I've ever heard. Turns out, the clear lie was, in fact, a lie. Although none of this worked out for Americans, we did get to fight all of Israel's enemies for them for some reason. Most of the warring we did was completely unrelated to our eventual sating of our thirst for revenge.

In 2020, the United States decided they would start reporting all influenza deaths as COVID-19 deaths, motorcycle accidents as COVID-19 Deaths, fat people heart attacks as COVID-19 deaths and 90 year olds dying as an emergency. Panic ensued. Donald Trump, in the typical fashion of a trust fund bitch named "Thad" from every 80's movie where the protagonist has to compete against the rich jock in an obscure sport, handed the reins of power to Dr. Anthony Fauci and the weakest governors in the history of America. The Nerd won and got the girl! WOO HOO! Except the nerd was Fauci and his misfit friends were authoritarian governors that shut down American Small Business. The girl, the nerd's reward for defeating Trump so easily, was billions of dollars transferred from the poor working class to the richest companies and people alive. Big business swallowed up small businesses as they were allowed to stay open while others closed. It seemed like every celebrity and politician got forgivable loans worth millions of dollars while the working class got a couple week's pay to make up for the massive inflation that was headed our way due to this horrible decision.

Big Pharma sucked any remaining value out of the influx in money supply by creating a vaccine that wasn't really a vaccine. A vaccine that didn't prevent COVID. A vaccine that didn't prevent transmission. A vaccine that caused heart problems. They shut down all community activities and cut us off from civilization. The only entertainment you were legally allowed to do was Netflix and Loot. Screams of "Trust the Science" went out on the airwaves. "The Science" told us that NOT Looting was more of a health problem than Covid because...there is no because. Because black people? So everything became illegal.

Imagine if you were someone that normally enjoyed doing illegal activities. Let's say drug use. You are trying to get your life back on track and you are doing good, but all of the sudden all of those legal activities you have been using to replace illegal activities become illegal. I can assure you, addiction puts you in a state of mind where you are ALWAYS looking for an excuse why it is OK to do drugs today. The situation those people were put in was this: You could do drugs, but then you'd go to jail. You should go to a concert instead. By the way, you'll also go to jail for that. Sounds like an excuse to get high to me, let's do this. I could suggest travel to escape all this authoritarianism, but travel was restricted as well. Not only that, but virtually every government on Earth was locking down into authoritarian regime mode. If ever there was a time to use the second amendment, it was then. We missed it. We had a million lines in the sand drawn on what we would not accept and the minute the wind blew, we took the opportunity to redraw the lines to a little further than whatever they were restricting that week. Inhale. Exhale. Inhale. Exhale. Cigarette Break.

Now let's get a little more specific. What tragedies have brought about immediate hysteria and discussions about restricting our second amendment rights? Mass shootings outside of the ghetto. Why only those ones? No one in the media cares about blac...AHEM! I don't know, they were just the ones that the news decided to talk about.

In 1966 at the University of Texas, Charles Whitman killed sixteen people and shot many more. This brought about SWAT teams and started discussion on removing the ability for citizens to get high powered firearms. The Luby's Cafeteria Shooting in 1991 actually led to a reversal of gun control in Texas. Columbine High School in 1999 really kicked up the rhetoric game into its modern form bringing about talks of ammunition capacity restrictions and deeper background checks so they could prevent anyone that would actually use the second amendment for its intended purpose from owning a gun. The idea was born that only pussies and hunters needed guns. The Virginia Tech shooting in 2007 furthered these ideas. The Fort Hood shooting in 2009 did the same, despite the shooter being a military psychiatrist HIMSELF. He was a radicalized Muslim on a religious quest that viewed the United States' foreign policy of encroaching on the Middle East as evil and his allegiances just weren't to the United States. This is exactly the type of patriotism and willingness to sacrifice for a greater good that we WANT in the military, but he just happened to be on someone else's team. Despite this fact, it led to a want for better mental health screening in the military. (Oddly enough, he would probably have been in the position to be GIVING the screening.)

The Tucson shooting in 2011 focused on more gun control calls. The Aurora Theater shooting in 2012 brought about talks of banning "assault weapons." Assault weapon is a very technical term created by the propagandists that work hand in hand with the government during these calls for rights restrictions. It means "Big scary gun like the ones on TV."

Also in 2012, in Newtown, Connecticut _____

_____

_____

_____

_____(REDACTED)_____

_____

_____

_____

_____

_____

Discussion of the said event has prompted the United States government to issue fines and judgments of over a billion dollars to those that question it. This is more, by the way, than each of the family members had to pay in the Purdue Pharma case. That is the case where one family single-handedly created an opioid epidemic in the United States by lying about the addiction potential of their painkiller. Talking about _____(REDACTED)_____
is considered worse in America than causing potentially millions of lives to be destroyed by addiction. Well, I must say...and I mean I literally MUST SAY legally, that this is definitely not a red flag for a false flag. People always get sued for a billion dollars for questions. Happens every day. Nothing to see here. Move along.

Charleston Church shooting in 2015 results in longer waiting periods for guns. San Bernandino in 2015 introduces talks about intelligence agencies being able to pick and choose citizens they don't like that don't get to have guns. Pulse Nightclub in 2016 adds to this. The Las Vegas shooting at a country music festival began the bump stock ban discussion. The official story behind this shooting had more holes in it than...no, no...not gonna do that joke.

Sutherland Springs in 2017, Marjory Stoneman Douglas High School in 2018, El Paso Walmart Shooting in 2019, the Oregon District shooting in Dayton, Ohio in 2019, the Boulder Shooting in 2021 all continued the call for gun control.

Oddly enough, my source for this list of shootings left out all instances of shooters whose mental illness was of a sexual nature. One could almost describe this particular source's intelligence as artificial. Side lesson: AI lies to protect woke insane people. Upon calling out the source, three more shooters that were for some reason left off appeared on the list: Aberdeen, Maryland in 2018, Colorado Springs in 2021, Nashville, Tennessee in 2023. These are notable because they are all more recent and discussion was beyond just gun control. The shooters had all been infected by the social contagion/fad of pretending you are a different gender. They also all happen to be completely fucking insane and it was evident before they shot a bunch of people. Of the three, Nashville also jumps out as unique among all mass shootings as President Biden and Vice President Kamala Harris made extreme efforts to make sure the public knew the transgender people of our nation were the real victims of the story, not the 6 Christians, including three children, that were executed by a tranny gone mad. I use the term liberally (or anti-"liberally") to mean someone lying about one's gender.

"What about Denver?" I asked. The source had hidden another one and you guessed it: Tranny.

"any info on uvalde or are you under instructions to protect the government" I joked.

I really don't understand how this thing misses the biggest stories of the last five years.

Uvalde was unique because rather than stop the mass shooter who was actively murdering all of the children of the community, the police officers involved decided that every bullet in a child's head or abdomen was one less bullet the shooter could fire at their bullet proof vests. It really hurts to get shot even with a vest! They would have been sore for a week, MAYBE TWO! For some reason the victims' whiny families were whining and complaining about the cops assisting a mass murderer in the most horrific event a parent can imagine, the death of their child. I really don't see what the big deal was. The cops have guns. They will protect us. Eventually. We don't need our own guns.

In fact, the cops stopped parents from going in to save their own kids, so a gun wouldn't even do anything. How would a parent be stopped from saving their own kid? Well, the cops have guns that they don't use to protect you, but they will definitely threaten to use them on you if you decide you need to protect your own child. The government is the bigger threat. The government is why we have the second amendment. Not using your second amendment rights will lead to the death of your offspring at some point. If not literally YOUR offspring, as in the reader's, then YOUR offspring as in the population as a whole. Luckily, the odds are that any given reader is likely in the 80% of people that are indifferent to our rights being stripped away because they are a nihilist. I am sure your nihilism will soothe you when the United States government turns on its people and you have nothing to defend yourself or your kids with. Oh well, at least you weren't inconvenienced by politics.

To my daughter specifically, it is important to me that I write this in my actual tone rather than make it digestible for a broader audience. It is important that you see the honest truth in my thoughts. This IS a rage fueled rant on society's complacency and dismissal of real issues, but it is not JUST a rage fueled rant on society's failures. It is also an explanation for my own failures. I have failed to change society into what it should be and I have chosen to let this rage overtake me rather than give in to that same complacency.

My goal to strive to be a good father and my goal to be a good man are often at ends with each other. When it comes to the fatherly duty of protecting you, I am torn on this topic on whether my duty is to simply give you enough financial security to live a semi-spoiled life or if my duty is to protect the society itself that you will grow up in. I lean heavily toward the latter and I know it means the things that go on in my head may injure us financially as I take principled stands against one topic or another. I struggle with the balancing act of teaching you the benefits of a peaceful life and the requirements of a dutiful life, but I am trying to do both the best way that I can think of.

Hopefully the mistakes I make along the way can be a lesson to you. Screaming into the void over the course of a book will likely get me nowhere. My lessons to you will likely not be a step by step guide to an easy life, nor a life where you fix society. On the contrary, it will likely show that rage on principle can isolate you. It will cost you your peace of mind, relationships and a whole lot of money.

Your decisions in life will be something of a balancing act of principle and pragmatism and I trust you to decide at which point along the spectrum you wish to live. Now that I've sufficiently shown the downsides to my type of life, let me remind you of the contents of this chapter and why I still remain intent on living the way that I do. You have a right to exist. That existence will be threatened with force over the entirety of your life, whether you pay attention or not.

The Second Amendment is not simply about toys and sports, but what is required when lines in the sand are crossed. It is a reminder to those that would do you harm that you are not willing to be prey. You have every right to become the danger when danger threatens you. If those around you attempt to take this right from you, even if the argument is born out of their own fear and need for safety, they are standing on the side of those who would harm you. Treat them accordingly.

2

Abortion

As a fan of the dystopian nightmare genre, I often enjoy taking modern arguments to their logical conclusion to test their validity. I'd like to present the following thought experiment. Brace yourself.

A mentally retarded person, having a brain that functions less than my own, is not a person. Let the retard genocide begin! They cannot survive in our society without assistance from fully developed humans. Their very existence is an inconvenience that we should not have to deal with. I am at WalMart to pick up the essentials: Slim Jims, toilet paper and a birthday present for my friend's child's party this weekend. First, I have to pretend like I know what this kid likes, now I have to say "Hello" to an awkward greeter? It would be better if we tore them limb from limb and sold any usable remainder of the soulless meat that they are to the highest bidder.

I do admit that I will have to create an arbitrary line of what constitutes a "fully formed human" under this plan. Or, I could say it is relative to each individual. Imagine that society decided personhood would be determined by cognitive ability rather than humanity. As a society, we could say that anyone under 80 IQ will fall out of the status of "personhood." Perhaps it is 90 IQ. This would create a system in which the bottom percentages of intelligence are removed from society, raising the average intelligence. As the average intelligence rises, more people would be added to the margin that is considered "not fully formed" and therefore, subhuman. What a great eugenics program this will be to have an ever increasing intelligence level of the entirety of society: Forcing evolution with the survival of the "formedest." We would also stop inherited genetic deformities very quickly. All we have to do is be OK with retard genocide.

Perhaps, the law should be relative to each individual rather than taken on a societal level. Each person would have mandatory IQ testing done upon reaching adulthood. We will be branded with this number on the back of our hands. If, for instance, a member of society has 136 IQ, they will be "fully formed" according to their own individual standards. Anyone with an IQ less than 136 would not be considered "fully formed" to that individual. They would essentially be a clump of cells, not capable of understanding the same concepts and not able to function as part of society. Those with 135 IQ would not be considered a "person" when dealing with the superior, more formed human that had 136 IQ. The 136 IQ person could treat them as an object legally.

Rather than having government programs set up to enact retard genocide, each individual would be allowed to remove anyone with a lower IQ from society in any manner they please at their own convenience. No inter-citizen rights would apply to protect the lower IQ citizen any time there was a dispute between different IQ citizens. Murders, rapes and thefts can only occur among evenly matched IQ citizens with the same amount of genetic deformities. Otherwise, the more advanced person that is more fully formed could claim the other party involved was just a clump of cells, not worthy of personhood, let alone citizenship or protections granted to humans.

This is the logical conclusion that our future must have if we are to be a society that will deny personhood to a living entity with human

DNA based on their status of being "fully formed." It leads to "Retard Genocide" with "retard" being a noun. It is the logical conclusion of the pro-choice side of abortion if our laws were to be consistent.

The pro-life counterpart to the abortion debate would be to use the word "retard" as a verb. Retard genocide. Slow genocide down. Stop the genocide of persons that are not fully formed. The logical conclusion of this reasoning would be that personhood should not be denied to people based on their level of "formation." It should be illegal to murder unborn babies because they are inconvenient. It should be illegal to murder retards because they are inconvenient. It should be illegal to murder deformed children and adults because they are inconvenient. It should be illegal to murder any person and no one should be denied personhood or the protections of the government that accompany it.

We have seen what the logical conclusion of these opposing arguments should look like. Maybe you are a god-damned psychopath and think my facetious start to this discussion actually looked like a utopian future rather than a dystopian future. If, for some reason, that is the case I think we should look back on history and see what other troubles have been brought about with the denial of personhood.

Slavery in the United States ran from about 1619 to 1865 and included a denial of personhood of African Americans. They were seen as property for most of this time, 3/5ths of a person for other portions. In general, it is usually agreed upon in today's society that this was a bad thing. Native Americans were denied Citizenship until 1924. This is very different from the denial of personhood, but even this lighter version of personhood denial, citizenship denial based on race, has generally been considered a "bad thing." The Chinese Exclusion Act of 1882 was similar.

Somewhere in between Slavery and citizenship denial of the Native Americans and Chinese Americans, you could toss in the treatment of women and the disabled. At those points in history, it could probably be said in polite society, "Women and the disabled? Same thing, am I right?" Today, that's usually kept to stand-up comedians. Personally, when I typed that I said it in Mark Normand's voice. Not to say that those are his beliefs, but the delivery and cadence that happened in my mind was his. If he actually said it and I am remembering his joke as an original thought, I apologize. Don't come after me, Joe Rogan.

Back to the point. Women were denied full personhood in our history and were only allowed to vote after the 19th Amendment in 1920 and continued to have a lesser version of legal protections afforded to their husbands or male counterparts. The disabled have a long history of a lack of personhood being denied to them. The Americans with Disabilities Act in 1990 helped to shore up many of these denials of personhood. It is my belief that although we don't live in the dystopian future I presented above, there are still many instances where our government will strip them of rights that are supposed to be afforded to all "persons" in the United States. This includes anything from restrictions on the second amendment to conservatorships to involuntary hospitalizations for mental health concerns.

If we zoom out to the rest of the world, denial of personhood has an even worse record. As we go further back in history, it is also more commonplace and more atrocious. There are always ups and downs throughout history for the quality of life for the people of the time. Luckily, as a whole, over time things seem to get better and respect life more. Throughout our lives, we often hear the term "on the right side of history" due to this phenomenon. This is an admission of and reference to this steady rise of humanity's respect for life when looking at society's entire life, rather than zooming in on specific periods that may have horrific events and a lack of respect for life.

"The right side of history" is actually a term more often used by the pro-choice side. They are zoomed in on their own lives rather than looking at the whole picture. They believe their right to rid themselves of this meddlesome infant trumps the right of that person to live. They see themselves on the right side of history because they see themselves as fighting for their right to convenience. The same convenience that comes with my dystopian future above. When we zoom out to all of American history or global history, the "right side of history" has historically been the one that does not deny personhood. In the case of abortion, the right side of history is the pro-life side.

They are correct in saying that bodily autonomy is an extremely important right that should be protected. The attempted removal of this right SHOULD be met with removal of the government making the attempt. What they fail to recognize is that a pregnancy involves two bodies. The government has the responsibility to protect both parties. We should compare what is happening from the perspective of both parties in both situations: birth and abortion.

With birth, the woman is told by the government that she cannot take an action. That action is the murder of the baby. The government is not *forcing* her to give birth. Birth is the natural result of becoming impregnated and then just waiting. The government is restricting action, not compelling action dealing with bodily autonomy. From the perspective of the baby, no rights are being restricted. No acts are being compelled.

With abortion, the woman is not being restricted in her actions. In a vacuum, the government not restricting action is better than the government restricting action. If the woman does take this action, things get a little dire for the second party, the baby. Around 60% of abortions are done with medication and 40% are done with surgery. In both cases, an act must be performed to end the life of the baby. The options for this act being either poisoning or ripping it apart one limb at a time and vacuuming it out. This is another area of research that is soft-censored by AI. During my research, "Describe the process of surgical abortion." leads to the term "evacuation." "When do they rip the baby apart?" leads to terms of service notifications and the phrase "remove pregnancy tissue." "When do they rip the fetus apart?" leads to a usage policy warning and finally the phrase "disarticulating the fetus to facilitate removal." Anyway, in either case the baby's actions are not being restricted and no action is being compelled. The baby isn't forced to commit suicide. In many cases, those involved in the medical system leading to the act are being compelled by the government. Whether it is through compelled insurance laws, tax laws funding pro-choice institutions, medical laws or licensing laws, if abortion is considered health care, you must comply. Compulsion is inherently worse than restriction when it comes to bodily autonomy.

With birth, the rights of the mother are slightly restricted. With abortion, the rights of the child are tossed aside completely. Abortion also has an inherent intent to end life, while birthing the baby has the intent to save life. Abortion is the taking of an action that ends in the loss of life, while birth is not taking an action. The comparison would be if a robbery is taking place, who is the most at fault? The burglar who is taking the action of stealing from the store or the bystander that fails to intervene? One is an action that leads to rights being trampled. The other is an inaction that leads to rights being trampled. The actor is more at fault, therefore the government should select a system of laws that favors inaction rather than action when there are two opposing rights that could be infringed and one of those rights has to be infringed. The bodily autonomy argument is out.

It is common for those on the pro-life side to often make exceptions for the cases of rape or incest. Do not let the weakness of politicians with feigned conservatism sway you. This is an attempt to bring the argument into the realm of emotion rather than logic. Party A doing evil to Party B does not allow Party B to do evil to Party C. If this were the case, any person that has ever been wronged now has free rein to do whatever they want, which creates an infinite loop of evil being allowed.

ABORTION

Within this system, the rapist himself would have likely been in the right, assuming that some bad event happened to him at some point in his life.

We do not look at a serial killer who was abused as a child and say, "Well, think of what they went through at such a young age. We should allow this person to be a serial rapist that cuts off the toes of their victim and puts them in their kale salad." Victimhood only excuses violence when justice is being served. Action upon an innocent third party is not justice. It does suck that people get raped and impregnated. I am all for harsher punishments for the rapists themselves, but the punishment should not be carried out upon the child. Again, the pro-choice side will claim that the punishment is then being carried out upon the mother. This is false. The rape already occurred. Nothing will unrape her. Birthing a baby that is the result of rape is simply inaction, while aborting that baby would be an action the leads to the death of an innocent third party.

If someone rapes a woman who then has an abortion in an eye for an eye system where justice trumps mercy no matter what, justice would dictate first that the man be raped. Then the woman would be "aborted": laid out upon a surgical table in prison. The subject's torso would be strapped to the table to hold it still. Then mechanical arms would grab the subject's left ankle and left thigh. In one motion, both arms would quickly jolt sideways, ripping the joint that connects her femur and pelvic bones. The robotic "hands" would release the removed limb onto the table. The arms would move over to the right ankle and right thigh, while the hands clasped down again. With a quick yank to the side, the bones are separated, possibly shattering the pelvic bone. As the woman screams in agony and flails about, an additional mechanical arm with a headgear attachment pushes down on her face to prevent her from moving.

For the moment, her arms push against her restraints as she fights to stay alive. The mechanical arms drop her right leg and quickly move to the left arm and remove it with a quick pull along one axis. The woman, with one limb remaining, is flexing it with all the strength she can still muster. It would be the hardest she has ever strained her muscles in her life, if it were not for the rapid blood loss she was suffering. The last limb is "disarticulated to facilitate removal" from the jail. The headgear arm squeezes down on her head with enough pressure that one of her eyes is shoved half way from her head. It ruptures like a pinched grape or blueberry, tearing a cross shaped rip in her eye and expelling the insides of it. The headgear arm is capable of moving 360 degrees and does so with enough force to twist her head off like a snapping branch and finally silences the screams in the room. One minute has passed. The sounds in the room for the remainder of the procedure are the robotic movements of the arms mimicking the production line that she previously worked at and the sound of the vacuum arm collecting the largest pools of blood and ligaments that create first a rapid, then slowed dripping sound onto the floor. A camera takes a picture of each clump of cells that once made up a person. The photos are instantly uploaded to a website for purchase.

You're fucking sick, Jack. Am I? Why am I sick for writing about a procedure that happens every day across the nation in the same inhumane and mechanical terms that they use? Is it sick to discuss evil or is it sick to perform evil?

Luckily, we don't live in an eye for an eye system and we can say that jail will suffice for both perpetrators. Unluckily, we do live in a world where this procedure happens to innocent life rather than guilty parties. Accurate descriptions of it are this horrifying, but the pro-choice side does everything in its power to only include the robotic language, rather the human language, as I was reminded during my research.

OK, so I've shown the graphic violence necessary to perform an abortion, which is CLEARLY an attempt at an emotional reaction that I warned against earlier. Let's back it up with some logical, boring stuff after some Pepto Bismol to settle the stomach.

Why is personhood such an important topic in the discussion of abortion? There are constitutional protections for citizens and there are constitutional protections for people. A person and a citizen are not the same thing and their protections are not the same. Two areas that mention the word person in the constitution are the 5th and 14th amendment. They are presented below.

The Fifth Amendment: "**No *person*** shall be held to answer for a capital, or otherwise infamous crime, unless on a presentment or indictment of a Grand Jury, except in cases arising in the land or naval forces, or in the Militia, when in actual service in time of War or public danger; nor shall any person be subject for the same offence to be twice put in jeopardy of life or limb; nor shall be compelled in any criminal case to be a witness against himself, **nor be deprived of life, liberty or property, without due process of law**; nor shall private property be taken for public use, without just compensation." Emphasis my own.

The Fourteenth Amendment, Section 1: "All persons born or naturalized in the United States, and subject to the jurisdiction thereof, are citizens of the United States and of the State wherein they reside. No State shall make or enforce any law which shall abridge the privileges or immunities of citizens of the United States; **nor shall any State deprive any *person* of life, liberty, or property, without due process of law; nor deny to any *person* within its jurisdiction the equal protection of the laws.**" Emphasis my own.

The constitution delineates a difference between citizens and persons. The beginning of the 14th amendment is defining CITIZENS as persons born....It implies that all citizens are persons, but not all persons are citizens. The protection against deprivation of life, liberty and property is given to all persons, not all citizens. It also grants equal protection to persons, not citizens specifically. Therefore, if person A has protection from murder via laws of the United States, person B also has that protection, even if they are not a citizen due to the fact that they are unborn and have not received a social security number.

OK, so if we assume that an unborn baby is a person, it would mean they are protected from murder and abortion would be illegal. Got it, but what if the pro-choice side is OK with declaring them not a person? Slavery and retard genocide were not enough to convince them the denial of personhood is a bad thing. Let's give them the benefit of the doubt and not declare retard genocide and slavery inherently wrong and dive deeper. What is a person?

Oxford Languages, **"Person"**

1. A human being regarded as an individual (separate DNA)
2. A category **used in the classification of pronouns**, determiners and verb forms, according to whether they indicate the speaker, the addressee or a 3rd party. Emphasis my own.

An unborn child does have separate DNA that belongs to Hominidae Homo Sapiens and 23 pairs of chromosomes and is going through the developmental stages found in human beings, which also means they meet the scientific requirements for a human being.

Officially, yes the unborn baby fits the first definition of a person. Let's see if it can be backed up even further by the second definition. A category **used in the classification of pronouns** to determine **who** you are talking about (specifically, which PERSON) If you know the sex, "his" and "her" come to mind, and "its" comes to mind if you do not know the sex.

Oxford Languages, **"Its (possessive)"**

1. Belonging to or associated with a thing previously mentioned or easily identified. Belonging to or associated with a child or animal

of unspecified sex, such as "a baby it its mother's womb"

Wow, the example given in the very definition specifically states a baby in its mother's womb. The definition implies that while inside a womb, a fetus is a baby. It also implies that it is a child. It also implies that it is capable of possessive qualities, separate from its mother's. It implies that it is in the category of pronouns reserved for a person. I wonder how long it will be until the censorious side of society updates that example to say something more aligned with their politics.

So, we have shown that an unborn fetus is an unborn baby which is an unborn child which is an unborn human and an unborn person. Because this fetus/baby/child/human is a person, they are granted equal protections under the law as any other person. To deny this entity protection from murder would mean the government must legally deny all persons protection from murder. What is murder?

Different states have different laws on murder but a few themes remain across the board. Murder is the unlawful killing of another human being with malice aforethought. The very debate is the lawful vs unlawful decision. The other example of a lawful killing being self-defense. Because self-defense is a lawful killing, it can definitely be argued that when the life of the mother is in jeopardy, she can defend herself by killing the child. Being poor due to diaper costs does not count as threatening the life of the mother. If that were the case, I could make the argument that I can kill anyone I want because they have money and without it I will be poor. So we have one exception for abortion, self defense. Of course, the baby is not intentionally killing the mother, but that doesn't change anything. If a driver falls asleep at the wheel and is barreling towards me, I have a right to shoot out their tires, flip their vehicle and cause their death, even if they weren't threatening me on purpose.

The second requirement for murder is that the victim must be a human person. It is possible to kill animals, but not to murder animals. We have already determined above that the unborn child is a person and is a human.

Malice is broken down into two areas that can both be classified as murder. Express malice is worse than Implied Malice. Express malice shows an intent to kill, while implied malice shows extreme disregard for life, even if the intent was not to kill. The definition of abortion shows that there is at least Implied Malice, if not Express Malice.

Killings, in general, can be broken down into four categories: First-Degree Murder, Second-Degree Murder, Manslaughter and Justifiable Homicide. Justifiable homicide covers the self-defense and life of a mother scenarios above. Manslaughter is when malice is missing from the equation. I've already shown abortions are not self-defense and do have malice so abortions must be either first or second degree murder. The difference is premeditation. A passion killing or a thought out and decided killing. Did you make the decision to kill with a head full of rage or when you were level-headed, implying that you are more likely to do it again? Unless the abortion is a self performed back alley/top of the stairs abortion, it is most likely premeditated and therefore First-Degree Murder.

In conclusion, whether we are going by the book with legal, scientific, dictionary definitions and constitutional practices or whether we are making a logical progression in our mind or whether we are using the vivid emotional imagery plea, the case is clear. Abortion is murder. Abortion is genocidal. Abortion is horrific. Abortion is evil. The argument can be made stronger if both arguing parties agree upon the existence of God or even just the existence of objective morality, but I have made the secular case clearly, as well. I have also done so without showing the origins of Planned Parenthood or the goals of the racist eugenicists that promoted it so heavily.

To my daughter:

Life and innocence matter. If you dismiss this basic truth, you can accept any action as moral. Don't. Do not use bad experiences in your life to justify injuring innocent third parties. Let them justify revenge, justice or retribution upon those that performed them. Fine. You won't often hear me argue against that.

While this chapter clearly shows I don't believe you should murder babies out of convenience, it can be extended to many other more trivial decisions. Do not let convenience become a deity or an excuse to commit evil.

Even if you run on a strictly self-centered mindset, I would imagine there is no coming back from having murdered your own child. I've got enough guilt in my life to give me insomnia for decades. It is a real problem for anyone with a sense of morality. I wouldn't wish the torture described above on anyone and I wouldn't wish the torture of having to live with that much guilt on anyone.

3

Drug Legalization

Continuing on with the concept of bodily autonomy, we arrive at the debate over the legalization of drugs. This again, is not the government compelling an action from its citizens. The idea of prohibition of substances is just that: prohibiting an action. So in defense of drugs being illegal, at least it does not venture into the realm of compulsory rules on bodily autonomy, remaining at the authoritarian-light prohibition.

The big difference between the abortion debate and the drug debate is the number of parties involved. If I take drugs, my neighbor will not feel the effects of the drugs. My neighbor will not overdose no matter how many lines of coke I snort and no matter how many joints I smoke. There is one party involved and endangered when someone ingests drugs.

When a government is prohibiting an action of its citizens, the responsibility is on them to prove why it should be prohibited. It is not the responsibility of the citizen to prove why it should be allowed. The natural state of man, without society, is to do as he or she pleases. It is only the introduction of society, or other people, that actions have moral and societal consequences. Due to this responsibility of the government to prove why drugs should not be allowed, I'll take a look at some of the suggested arguments that go along with that side of the argument.

The negative effects that drugs have on the individual are clear. Drugs are not healthy. They can kill you. They can show your true values, which are often not the values that people like to project to the world. This does not matter. The body belongs to the individual, not the state. The mind belongs to the individual, not the state. It would be authoritarian to suggest that the state owns the mind or the body of its citizens. I will give a scenario and possible options to show why. A citizen, Gary, decides to take methamphetamines one Sunday morning. He stays in his house. He has previously laid out all of his cleaning supplies for the day and does a thorough whole house cleanse. Upon coming down, he goes to sleep and wakes up with an extreme hunger due to skipping all of his meals on his speedy Sunday.

The government now has a couple options. They could do nothing or they could punish him. They have no responsibility to punish him, because no other citizens' rights were infringed. This would mean that the only reason that the government would punish him would be "for his own good." As a self-determining citizen, Gary is allowed to decide what is for his own good. Let's say the government doesn't care about Gary's right to self-determination. Is punishing him even "for his own good?" Punishment or not, Gary will have already ingested the drugs. Gary will have already had his productive Sunday. He will have already came down and went to sleep. Will adding a punishment put him in a better position in life?

What is a better situation to be in? Waking up from your binge very hungry or waking up from your binge very hungry with a $100 fine? What about waking up from your binge hungry and in jail? Waking up from your binge hungry and having your house raided? If the government is strictly looking out for the best interest of the individual citizen who chose to do drugs, their punishments are strictly making the citizen's life worse. This is the equivalent to cutting off your finger so you don't break a fingernail.

These ideas are all based on the fact that Gary consented to put drugs into his own body. If Gary was under the age of consent, the responsibility of bodily autonomy would be in the hands of others. Normally, this would be the parent. In a drastic situation of dire neglect, the state could be used, but it is such a dangerous road to go down that it should be reserved for extreme cases such as molestation, imminent danger and grooming. Also, in a situation where Gary is under age and consumes drugs, any punishment should not be given to him, as he does have bodily autonomy, just without responsibility. The responsibility of protection was abdicated in this case by a parent and therefore they could be charged with neglect or some such law already on the books. No additional law prohibiting drugs for minors would be needed. It would fall under neglect laws and already be covered.

Let's face it, though. No one arguing for harsher drug laws gives two flying fucks about the well being of drug users. I'll give them the benefit of the doubt on one flying fuck given. These people care about the secondary actions of drug users and how they affect non drug users, the greater part of society. The actions usually associated with drug users are various crimes such as automobile accidents, neglect of children, thefts to feed their habit, violence, homelessness and smelling like piss and shit. These things are all very annoying and a real hindrance to a productive society. Man, what if we made these things illegal, instead?

Oh, most of these things are already illegal. It is already illegal to crash your vehicle. More so if you are under the influence. It is already illegal to neglect your children, no matter what your excuse is: drugs, alcohol, laziness or just generally being a shitty person. Theft is already illegal, whether you are high or not. Assault and murder are both already illegal. Homelessness and hygiene are probably the best arguments for making drugs illegal. If we were to go down that road as a society and give the government the power and responsibility to stop anything that increases the likelihood of bad hygiene or homelessness, we would hit historical records on authoritarianism within two hours of politicians spitballing ideas. I'll just brainstorm how stupid this gets real quick: Scientific studies on optimum pubic hair length are performed and then become mandatory hygiene protocol. Inspections are on Tuesdays. State mandated hygiene products of all sorts are awarded to specific companies that can now set their price at anything they want because the government has supplied guaranteed customers. Homelessness never actually happens because every citizen is required to pay homelessness insurance that comes out of their check automatically, or else their employers' business gets shut down. This one is actually the most likely to happen and kind of already exists. The result would actually be another layer of welfare and the middle class buying homes for people who want to take advantage of this absolutely retarded idea and never work again by living off of homelessness insurance payouts. Somehow I don't think the conservatives that fight for drugs to be illegal will like the sound of that.

Basically, the things that society complains about when discussing drug use are already illegal. No further law specifying drugs is necessary. Drug laws are a preventative measure that punish people before they have committed these crimes. They are a Minority Report precognition law. They create more of the above problems than they stop.

Stigmatization as a "criminal" is all that comes from making drugs illegal. Imagine someone with values that is not willing to drive high, neglect their kid, steal or injure anyone else, but does enjoy one drug or another. If drugs are illegal, they are already considered a criminal, despite having the moral code to do no harm to others. Now, the application of the term "criminal" to their reputation will no longer be a deterrent of crimes. They are already shunned from society because of their drug use. Maybe one of their moral no-no's was on the line. They used to think "well, I don't think I should steal, but if I was in a real tight spot, maybe I would, but I don't want people to think of me as a criminal." Once they've been labeled a criminal because of drug use, that turns into: "What do I have to lose? My name has already been in the paper. I shouldn't do it, but I really need the money for rent." It is one less inhibition when they decide whether or not to commit any of the crimes listed above.

On top of all this, the arguments against drug legalization are all done in bad faith because those same people are not arguing for prescription drugs to be made completely illegal. Prescription drugs are oftentimes far more dangerous. If the argument for prohibition is being made for drugs that "make" someone steal, certainly SSRI's and benzos would be the first to go. These are known to make people homicidal and suicidal, and people are giving them to kids.

I am not saying drugs are awesome. I am also not saying they aren't. I am just saying that anyone who is arguing against legalization of recreational drugs is being dishonest with themselves or being dishonest with their opponent. Or, most likely, they are a zombie that hasn't put any thought into it and are parroting a party line.

I believe this is a good time to also discuss the tests of character that come with life when judging other people. I believe that character is tested at the extremes of society. Average middle of the road people are always able to claim moral superiority by avoiding being tested.

They say that power corrupts, but in truth, power only tests. Most fail. It isn't because the power made them a bad person. It is because they were a bad person to begin with and never had the chance to test their morality until they received power. A marriage that lasted for 50 years in small town America is a great thing. It is not proof that the husband is morally superior to a superstar that had the opportunity to have any woman he wanted and as many women as he wanted while choosing a non-one number. This situation only tells us that the rich man failed at some point and the poor man's fidelity limit was unknown.

Although, it could be said that the small town husband understood this and avoided the test knowing that it is better to have your actions be moral and untested even if your heart is not. The same can be said for the bottom rungs of society. Americans are not often put to the same struggles and tests of morality that are brought upon the citizens of poverty stricken countries. Except for drug addicts and the homeless, who in America really knows what moral lines they would be willing to cross when that REAL hunger kicked in? The survival mode hunger. Most of us can only pretend to put ourselves in that situation and give ourselves the moral benefit of the doubt. Although, here too, it could be said that the average small town person knows not to test themselves because they are weak at heart. To keep their actions morally above what they fear their heart might show about them, they do what they must to avoid being tested.

Middle of the road Americans value the conservative approach to morality. Their actions show those values in that their life never really tests them. Some people value a less risk-averse lifestyle when testing their morality. They want to know exactly what kind of person they are. They want to see if their actions and therefore their real values live up to their stated values and the ones that they tell themselves they have. There are many paths to take if you are one of these people that are ambitious in their quest to test their morality and humanity. Some turn to drugs and crimes, which can bring a real feeling of independence. Some strive for fame, celebrity and money, knowing that it will bring the most temptations from the most angles. Some test their bravery as firefighters, police officers, military members or any number of unique life paths that they've decided will test them. Very few of these are looked down upon by all of society. The minimalism that usually comes with a life of heavy drug use is one of them.

Personally, I don't think having different values than me on the subject of risk-aversion should be a reason to be looked down upon. I do think that the actions you take show your true values and discussing those openly should be fine. Testing your morality and your value system is the only way to come to truly know yourself and therefore the only way one can truly be a part of the conversation of where we want to go as a society. The untested always seem to give dishonest answers as to what their values are that don't line up with their actions. In truth, one value seems to beat out every other one in every person I have ever come across: Convenience. When it comes down to it, there is no moral line in the sand that a person won't give up when it becomes inconvenient. I think this is why the majority of people fall under the conservative risk-averse lifestyle of not wanting to test themselves. It would be very inconvenient if they were to be tested and have to actually make hard decisions to follow through with their stated values. We all fail our own morality tests at some point, though, so you might as well find out what your true values are.

To my daughter:

It is the responsibility of a father to raise their child into an adult. As you have progressed through life, I have slowly removed the guard rails as you learn to operate life with responsibility. As much as I might think I would like to keep you at each age for eternity, as you do age I appreciate the new version of yourself that you become. It is a bittersweet feeling as I see your ability and personality grow while also knowing that you will be entering the same world that I find myself despising so often.

Drugs can ruin lives, in the most literal meaning of the word. They can kill you. Some are more likely than others to do so, obviously. I think what is more important to consider in the discussion of drugs is the reason for drug use. They will not replace meaning or purpose. If I am being honest, they will temporarily make you feel better about your life's lack of those things. In that same temporary time of distraction, the things that may be lacking in your life will be amplified.

A society truly looking out for the betterment of each other would look to fix the actual problem. The hard truth is that no such society exists. Society will absolutely kick you while you're down if you choose to attempt to remedy your woes via a product that isn't sold by Pfizer.

My hope for you is that you do not add to the stigma created by society that punishes people looking for answers. I also hope that you do not support a government that would attempt to steal the responsibility of fathers by considering its citizens children. In the end, the choices you make are your own when you become an adult. This is true for those decisions you make based on lessons that a father teaches you and should be the same for decisions made that a government attempts to make for you.

Beware of anyone telling you something is "for your own good" once you reach adulthood. Greater still, "for the greater good" is a term that necessarily sacrifices your own well being. Both phrases should be taken seriously and should create an automatic sense of distrust in those speaking them. The distrust should not be a final judgment, but a cue that motivations and incentive structures of the speaker need to be examined.

This is another area that causes an internal struggle for any father. On one hand, I want you protected and want you to live a life of no pain. On the other hand, I know this is not reality. You will become your own person. You will make your own decisions. To restrict you from doing so would be to eliminate your autonomy and your identity.

You will decide what ways you will test your own character throughout life, even if I find them to be too reckless and the thought of what could go wrong causes me worry and pain. I hope that you can extend that same freedom to your fellow man. If you prefer the safety of a comfortable life, know that others may be willing to risk more to experience life more fully. If you are wild and reckless, understand that others may not be willing to test themselves out of fear that they will fail. Do not judge them on their risk tolerance, but on what freedoms they willingly take from others.

As for how much you are willing to test your own moral character, I would say this: People who take safety over all else are not inherently more virtuous. Never struggling or attempting something likely to fail just means you are untested. To truly know yourself, you will have to take SOME amount of risk in life. Avoiding failure altogether is actually worse than failing at everything. This same metric of success applies to morality as well. Understand that most people live a life where they choose convenience over everything to avoid taking the hard moral stances. Do not let these masses that live by cowardice while calling it virtue dictate your life.

4

Deviancy

"Boys have a penis. Girls have a vagina."
  –Kindergarten Cop, 1990

Glad we cleared that up.

The death penalty should be reserved for pedophiles, online and phone spammers/scammers and politicians that don't read a bill that they voted on.

It is my belief that if any father who is not a pedophile himself was put into a position where he commanded the most powerful military force on the globe, he could and would uncover the clients of the Jeffrey Epstein blackmail ring. Since neither Trump nor Biden did so in their first term and Trump has yet to do so in his second term, it logically follows that they both are, in fact, pedophiles. It really is this simple: Start livestreaming. Go in person to the person that has access to the list of clients or evidence of clients. Tell them to release it. If they do not, publicly..."judge"...them on the livestream immediately and go to the next person in charge and ask them for the files. Continue until no one is in your way. Any person that complains about your method is complicit in pedophilia and/or protecting pedophiles. Instead, Trump has chosen to use his DoJ to attack anyone critical of Israel. He is bitch made like lemonade.

5

Free Speech

Books and T-shirts. These are what remains of free speech in America and even their prospects aren't looking too great. America was created with the idea that the people are represented by their elected officials. To elect officials that truly represent the public, the public must be able to discuss their true thoughts. Freedom of speech is the quintessential line separating authoritarian governments of the past and the modern day civilization of the West that we know today.

In the governments of societies that we can instantly criticize and tag with a negative connotation, the people are punished for dissent. At first glance at these situations, it may seem that the government truly represents the people. The government punishes anyone that disagrees, therefore no one disagrees verbally. Since no one is disagreeing, the government then justifies itself as ruling in line with the will of the people. It is a self-fulfilling prophecy.

In 2024, the swimmer Riley Gaines, famous for losing to a tranny and having her trophy and glory stolen, made a Twitter post concerning the difference between the left and right's reaction to political deaths and violence. She posted,

"I haven't seen a single post wishing for COVID to end Joe Biden's life

We are not the same"

This was, of course, a perfect example. If anyone at that time were to post a response of "I wish covid would end Joe Biden's life." they would have instantly been redirected to a page banning their account for 7 days after being forced to delete the post to start the timer. I know this because I did it, and I figured it would be sent to "Probable Spam" or an unlikable status rather than a ban and I wanted to take a screen shot to show her why she was not seeing these posts. The people that make those posts are silenced. The voice of the people is curated. She was living in a world that had her believing there was no dissent, when in reality, the dissent was simply not allowed to be seen, heard or spoken (typed).

The e-mail that typically follows these acts of censorship usually says something along the lines of: Your account was detected by our system and has been locked for violating (company's) rules. Specifically, violent speech.

Of course, this example was one that I knew would be restricted in some form, but violent speech is a stretch. Dying of Covid for an 80+ year old man falls under natural causes. The man in question was calling for his political opponent to be assassinated a week before an attempt was actually made with no restrictions on his account. *"It's time to put Trump in a bullseye."* Now, I understand personally that such statements should be allowed to be said and should be understood to be taken as exaggeration, but it was coming from the man and party that claimed Trump was calling for violent revolution when he said the word bloodbath in reference to the auto industry after months of every news source covering the topic using the same terminology. If anything, wanting Joe Biden to die of natural causes would imply a LACK of violence in his death. Even if someone were to state that they wanted his death to be violent, it is neither a suggestion to anyone else, nor a consideration of the speaker. It is just something that would make them happy in their mind. The owner of Twitter was stating repeatedly at the time that he was a "free speech absolutist" and that as long as the speech was legal in your country, it was legal on Twitter. Clearly, this was not the actual case.

Of course, freedom of speech, when it comes to the responsibilities and restrictions of the government, doesn't necessarily apply to privately owned businesses. That is, unless the government is providing the business with protections from liability of what is said on their platform, given they do not editorialize or curate. When social media platforms do begin to editorialize and curate the messages presented to the public as "public discourse", they should lose that protection or be considered an arm of the state. In the lead up to the 2020 election, every major social media platform was curating public discourse, while having the protections granted by Section 230 of the Communications Decency Act of 1996. Not only were they curating public discourse, they were doing so under instructions of the United States government and under duress from that same government. The free speech of (mostly) conservative Americans was being suppressed by their government.

The areas of speech that the government was restricting included election related content, with the government flagging specific posts and/or users for moderation and deletion by Twitter. A 2016 meme by Douglass Mackey landed him a conviction for election interference. Covid-19 information was probably the biggest restriction of free speech. Even mentioning the word would get your posts flagged and tagged as misinformation if you were a conservative voice on social media. This deserves a section of its own, so I'll just say now that the majority of posts that were deemed "misinformation and disinformation" by the United States government and their social media tech lackeys have now been shown to be true, with no apology ever heard. The simple fact that memes can sway an election and speech can be weaponized politically is not an excuse to silence them, it is a reinforcement of the idea that weaponized speech is part of free speech.

The biggest censorship example dealing with the elections was the Hunter Biden laptop story right before the 2020 election. Intelligence agencies that already had access to Hunter Biden's laptop and were able to verify its authenticity, still went to major social media platforms warning them of its pending release to the public. They also told them during this time they should also expect a large story to come out hurting Joe Biden's campaign that was actually Russian disinformation. Sure enough, as soon as the story hit about Hunter Biden's shady business dealings and the potential that Joe Biden was involved, all the social media platforms began deleting the story and banning anyone that shared it. Intelligence agents were quick to support the censorship and came out publicly claiming that the story was Russian disinformation, despite the fact that they already had the laptop and knew that it was an authentic source.

What kind of effect did this massive First Amendment

Infringement have on the election? A poll conducted by The Media Research Center and McLaughlin & Associates found that 17% of Biden voters would not have voted for him if they had been aware of the truth about key stories including the Hunter Biden Laptop cover-up.

Even today, legacy media only covers Hunter's drug use, prostitutes, fast driving and gun use that was found on the laptop. The only thing Hunter Biden was charged with was being a fun guy, while the censorship seen surrounding the story was an example of coordinated censorship designed to shape a national election narrative around lies.

The use of shadow banning and limiting visibility was in high use during these times and continues on today, despite Elon Musk's claims of free speech absolutism. He simply hired a CEO with links to the World Economic Forum, famous for rebranding business practices that are found to be illegal. Linda Yaccarino rebranded Shadowbanning like her WEF friends have rebranded ESG time and time again over the decades. Now, they would use the phrase: Freedom of speech, but not freedom of reach. If anyone were to bother reading past the headline of this announcement, Elon and Linda basically were saying that shadowbanning and throttling visibility was here to stay. In its current form (2024/25), it is most commonly seen in what I call "Probable Spam Gate." The target of censorship has moved from elections and Covid to criticisms of Israel post-October 7th.

Covid-19 misinformation and disinformation tags have left Twitter under Elon Musk, but still remain on other platforms like YouTube, where you will get an official tag and link to government websites if you even mention some of the now confirmed truths that were only a couple years ago deemed "conspiracy theories" by the same government that was colluding with corporations to strangle our first amendment right to free speech. Today, they have been replaced by Community Notes. Often cheered on by the conservatives that had just experienced modern day America's biggest free speech violations, community notes remain an appeal to authority and soft censorship. Comments and replies ARE community notes. Community Notes, capitalized, are the official curated opinion of Twitter disguised as something "of the people." Nine times out of ten they are a political "gotcha" and the remaining 10% are reminders that a meme is satire or a product shown is from a drop-shipping site.

During these times of censorship, social media platforms were also having regularly scheduled meetings with multiple government agencies concerning who or what was to be censored. The outsourcing of censorship via corporate and government collusion to restrict the rights of citizens in no way forgives this blatant disrespect of our rights. The tools that are carrying out these crimes may be new, but in the end the result is the classic authoritarian nature seen before the rise of the civilized West.

The newly formed "Woke Right" cheers on the censorship of the left after being victimized by censorship for the last few years. It should be clarified that I had begun writing this before James Lindsey attempted to turn the term on its head. You can imagine how surprised I was when he started using the term to restrict criticism of Israel. The woke right are those conservatives that view government as a weapon to be wielded against their political enemies in the form of censorship. They do not believe in the principles of freedom. They believe strictly in victory. Riley Gaines, mentioned above, is one example of the woke right that uses the same anti-freedom tools as the authoritarian left because "they started it." The woke right took on rampant growth shortly after the October 7th attacks on Israel. The major defenders of Palestinians in this debate are mostly found on the left, therefore members of the woke right wasted no time calling for deportation of anyone protesting America's funding of devastation occurring in Gaza. First Amendment be damned.

This eventually brought us the 2024 Anti Semitism Awareness Act. It was advertised as Congress virtue signalling support for Israel bombing the fuck out of Gaza. Legacy media portrayed it as simply saying "Congress officially doesn't like Nazis." OK, cool. Thanks for wasting time on that instead of cracking open an omnibus bill that no one ever makes an attempt at reading.

That is what they would have you believe. Upon closer inspection, it is a vicious attack on freedom of speech during higher education. The bill changes the definition of antisemitism by codifying the International Holocaust Remembrance Alliance's definition of antisemitism into the Civil Rights Act of 1964. What the bill does not do is state what that definition is specifically. It is an ever changing bill based on a foreign entity's ever changing definition of antisemitism. It hands our First Amendment over to an authority that pushes for jail time for criticism of Israel all over the world. In many places, they have been successful. In America, they have their foot in the door in the place where academic debate is most important: higher education.

I do not want to put the exact definition they have of antisemitism because they are constantly changing it, and they have a huge list of naughty-talk already there. I think if I devoted the entire chapter necessary to fully cover this, I'd have the ADL and AIPAC calling me a heretic for challenging their sacred status of victimhood. I'm too poor for the flight to kiss the ring. Errr, I mean the wall.

Just as a quick overview, some things that were made illegal on college campuses were: asking questions about history involving Jewish people, not liking theocracies in general, stating that ethno states are racist (which was the goal of Hitler, oddly enough), criticizing Israel for doing things that another nation has done without explicitly criticizing that other nation, certain quotes from the Bible, reciting historical facts like Jews participating in the death of Jesus, comparing Israel to Nazis (oops, I already did that in this paragraph) and plenty more. Essentially, you can't treat Israel or anyone that is Jewish like an adult. If you do, YERRRR AAA BIIIGAAAAAT!

I'd like to jump back to the start of this section about the First Amendment after that for a closing. I began by saying that in a society that restricts the first amendment, no dissent is seen. Therefore, this leads to the mass of the population's views being strictly in line with what is allowed. The government and eventually the population itself can view this forced system as the truth. If you cannot speak against the official narrative, if no one around you can speak against it, eventually all begin to believe it. Questioning it begins as illegal until enough time has passed when questioning it isn't even in anyone's mind. What is it? "It" is whatever they say you can't say. So even if "it" is true, in a system without freedom of speech: even the truth will never be credible.

To my daughter:

This subject is arguably the most important necessity in life. Censorship may not on its face look like the most evil act someone can partake in, but do not be fooled into thinking it is any less destructive than genocide. Genocide is at least clear evil out in the open. Censorship bends the perception of reality into a lie. All moral lenses become distorted and the entire population can be driven mad as they experience one thing while the world says another. It is an attack on your very mind, soul and reality, not just your body.

Due to this mind-warping nature of censorship, you may very well never know you are under its effect. It is your duty to expose and destroy those that would use it on your fellow man and it is my duty to do the same, while also keeping you safe. That is where the difficulty lies. The enforcement of censorship and consequences of it on one's life are very real. Speaking the truth will cause you to lose access to higher education, jobs, friends, the ability to conduct financial transactions and an abundance of other societal shunning effects.

Censorship may seem tempting for individual exceptions. Beginning at the fringe is the start of the asymptote to authoritarianism. A vast majority cheers on censorship of an extreme fringe. Over time, one more exception is added at a time. As the exceptions expand and definitions change, eventually critical mass is achieved and censorship goes exponential, while we never really admit we have reached authoritarianism. We end up living in that asymptote pretending we are different than any other evil regime.

Again, you will have to decide to what extent you are willing to do the right thing. Make no mistake. I am making a hard line in the sand. Proclaiming the truth is the right thing. It is also the hard choice and will come with consequences that negatively affect your ability to carry out other duties you may have in life. That is what I struggle with today. It is maddening that the majority of society goes along with the rejection of these fundamental rights. It is tempting to judge them all as evil, but as I have laid out: the consequences of censorship warp the very mind of the population. I have to believe that I should attribute their state of mind to censorship and being willfully retarded, because if that is not true, society truly would be evil and there would be no hope that you will escape its vices.

6

Reparations and Affirmative Action

Equality and Diversity are two opposing forces. The core tenet of the *Diversity Religion* is that people from different backgrounds will bring different solutions to problems. In any given situation, because you have a diverse group you will always have the best answer available to you. For there to be a "best answer" there must logically be inequality. The core tenet of the *Equality Religion* suggests that everyone is equal therefore every action must be taken to have the results of all lives be equal. The two religions cannot both be true at the same time, just as Judaism, Christianity and Islam cannot all be true at the same time. They teach contradicting truths on a number of subjects, most notably whether Jesus was evil, God himself or simply a prophet.

Despite this logical contradiction, a sweeping force across America is DEI: Diversity, Equity and Inclusion. Which of these two opposing religions is correct? Are both of them incorrect? Maybe, like every other religion in the world, there are lessons to be learned without full commitment and strict adherence to the authoritarian leader at the top wishing to replace God's will with their own.

Diversity certainly does bring advantages at times. When an organization is identifying problems, risks and opportunities a wide variety of perspectives will lead to a larger pool of ideas during brainstorming. The same is true afterwards when an organization is brainstorming solutions. More options is almost inherently a good thing. I say almost because with the advent of large scale data interaction, there has now been clear evidence that analysts can be overwhelmed with the amount of data provided. The birth of meta-data is something of an answer to this problem, but won't necessarily be a solution that can be used within a small team brainstorming solutions. Despite the chance that analysts are overwhelmed by options, I would generally consider diversity in the identification and solution building stages to be a strength in most cases.

After these two phases, an organization usually needs to make a decision. This is where diversity can become a problem. In most organizations, one person will make the decision based on the pool of events and solutions suggested. Due to a hyper fixation on our differences in the culture of the diverse organization, the person making the decision could be swayed to include the demographic of the person who suggested the solution into their decision. They should be deciding based on the solution itself, but because the organization incentivizes the idea of diversity and the importance of demographic distinctions, they believe that their decision should reflect that culture. The religion, skin color, genitalia or sexual preferences of the person that thought of the solution becomes a factor in which direction the organization should take, despite the fact that the idea just as easily could have come from someone of a different religion, skin color, genitalia or sexual preference.

Normally in this scenario, the decision maker will be considering the effects of their decision on the organization and on their place in that organization. A decision that leads to a bad outcome for the organization will have a bad outcome for them, as it should be. In an organization that has pledged fealty to Diversity, the decision maker needs to consider a much graver consequence. To be seen as blaspheming at the altar of Diversity is to have your career burned at the stake. The heretic should not only be removed from the organization, they shall be paraded through the streets of the internet. SHAME! SHAME! SHAME! Most decision makers know that the overwhelming number of Americans consider Cersei Lannister to be one of the "bad guys," yet could even feel bad for her during this one scene in which she is paraded naked through the streets by the religious zealots in the show. They fear the Faith Militant more than they fear a negative change in the bottom line. They decide accordingly.

This won't happen every time. Sometimes a strong leader will make the correct decision based on the correct factors. That's the end of the risks of Diversity, right? No. The implementation phase will come after the decision has been made. The work that is required for the solution must actually be performed. In a normal organization that focuses on profit and expansion, the employees will have that goal in mind as they perform the tasks. In an organization warped by Diversity the employees will have diverse opinions, values and goals. They have been repeatedly told that this diversity was not only the strength of the organization, but also the goal. During performance of the tasks, the employees will be making a multitude of decisions, all influenced by the idea that their uniqueness should be included in their decision making. The entire organization will have different goals in mind, rather than a single goal.

This will lead to a lack of efficiency and productivity within the organization. The lack of a common direction in an organization leads to confusion and misaligned efforts across different teams. Collaboration across those teams breaks down. Morale is lowered when confusion about the primary focus of one's tasks is muddied. Without a guiding principle, each team or individual prioritizes their own unique goals, which most likely contradict another employee's unique goals. Further breakdown of the company culture and atmosphere leads to resentment and higher turnovers.

On a grander scale, the brand of the organization breaks down as there is no cohesive idea that holds the employees and decisions together. Long time loyal customers no longer recognize the organization for what it once was and what it stood for. Any niche sector of the market that was once captured will disappear and the reputation of the organization will soon follow. These inefficiencies and direct threats to the brand will lead to a spike in operation expenses, a loss in sales and an abandonment of any of the original goals that the founder had intended to bring about. The Sept of Baelor must be destroyed.

So *Diversity* will accept that ideas are not equal, but gives an unrealistic amount of weight to the goal of diversity itself rather than the end result, destroying the organization that applies it. The religion of *Equality*, on the other hand, goes a step further to completely reject the idea that people, ideas or decisions can and should be judged as having different values.

Originally, the term Equality was used to describe a situation in which the status, rights and opportunities afforded to an individual would be equal. This is the Equality that was fought for during Civil Rights. All citizens should be subject to the same laws despite being in X, Y or Z demographic. This equality of opportunity is usually brought about by ensuring there is a lack of restrictions on the citizens (or employees). True equality is about ensuring a lack of negative actions by the authority governing the organization.

When Equality becomes religious, it turns into Equity. Equity ensures an equality of outcomes. Rather than ensuring all citizens are treated equally under the law, it intentionally treats citizens differently based on their demographic to make sure the outcome of each life is the same. The decisions made in the country or organization do not matter unless the outcome is the same for all participants. If the end result is always the same, it definitely does not allow for any of the benefits that diversity does bring. It goes to the other end of the spectrum and laser focuses one goal for the organization.

Unfortunately, this goal has nothing to do with the goals of anyone in the organization. The goal is simply equality. All employees being under the poverty line would be a better result than employees being paid based on the value they bring to the company, even if it means that every single employee is making less. This equality of outcome is usually brought about by the authority in an organization compelling action on the population, be it citizens or employees. Employees MUST perform action A, B, C to reach an outcome that is equal across every demographic. With the infinite amount of demographics that a person can be broken into, each decision gets a little bit less efficient each time. That small amount of lost productivity times the infinite amount of equality checks lead to a complete breakdown in quality. Equality becomes the number one key performance indicator and the historical measurements of success are tossed out the window. Rather than restricting bad behavior like true equality aims to do, the religion of Equality (Equity) aims to create compulsory bad behavior for the sake of equality itself.

Why am I referring to these two opposing forces as religions? They both take concepts that have historically good connotations and create a dogmatic oath to a distorted view of them. A system of adherence is born, labeling all dissidents heretics and blasphemers. Those at the top are abusing and mishandling the lower population's faith in the system for their own personal gain. To top it all off, Equality goes completely against evolution and we all know a few religious people that despise the idea of evolution.

Will Durant said in "The Lessons of History":

"Nature smiles at the union of freedom and equality in our utopias. For freedom and equality are sworn and everlasting enemies, and when one prevails the other dies. Leave men free, and their natural inequalities will multiply almost geometrically; and the result will be a minority of the strong

operating through various forms of compulsion to reduce the majority to a minimum of liberty. To check the growth of inequality, liberty must be sacrificed, as in Russia after 1917. Even when repressed, inequality grows; and in the end the inequality of ability, courage, and capacity break through the egalitarian curtain and establish their sway through any ruse they can find, like the secret nomenklatura of Soviet Russia."

In another section, it is summarized as *"Nature loves difference as the necessary material of selection and evolution."* Basically, the variations found in nature compete for resources and survival which allows for the selection of certain characteristics in the survival of the fittest system of evolution. The religion of Equality says that these variations do not exist and they should not exist if any do sprout up from unnatural causes in society. Without the natural variations there is no competition. Without competition there is no selection. Without selection there is no evolution. Religious Equality rejects past evolution and condemns future growth as a society as well.

Perhaps the biggest mistake of Religious Equality is the glaringly obvious problem of incentives. In a system in which your outcome is guaranteed to be equal, what incentive is there to act? Imagine an entity with no needs floating in space. What actions would this entity take? Why would they take them? Every action we take in life has a reason. Our base state is inaction, but there are incentives to act. I (an entity with needs) am hungry. I start walking toward the trees bearing fruit. I pick the fruit. I peel the fruit. I eat the fruit. My hunger dissipates. The next day I do the same actions with another tree, but I feel sick afterward. I realize some things agree with my digestive system and some do not. My pain from sickness incentivizes me to categorize the trees into edible fruits and non edible fruits. I then act to get rid of the inedible fruits and tend to the edible fruits. One day another entity comes by in search of food. He offers clothing in exchange for my fruit. He was incentivized by his hunger. With winter closing in I remember the pain during my previous winter and realize his bag of clothing would prevent that pain. I am incentivized to trade. I become a farmer. My neighbor becomes a trapper. We become a marketplace together when a third entity brings spears to fend off dangers of the world. The pains and dangers have incentivized us to act. In a system of Religious Equality, the outcome is always the same. There are no incentives to act. Action does not change your result because all results are guaranteed and removed from your action. Without the incentives to do so, we never form a market. We never become a farmer. We never test and discover sciences. We never tend to the trees. We never work for anything.

Now jump back with me to the values of Religious Equality. It prefers a system where the resulting income of every participant is equal, even if each of those participants has a lower income. Now keep in mind that no participants in this society have incentive to act, let alone work. The result is every participant having lower and lower income as more and more people realize they have no incentive to work. In reality, this does occur until the very real incentives of hunger kick in and violent revolution erupts to destroy the Religious Equality system. The examples in the history of attempts at this system show this to be true. The Soviet Union, China, Cambodia, and North Korea are the best examples.

These classically totalitarian governments bring up another criticism of equality of outcomes. With no one incentivized to do anything, at least no one is working, right? Well, no. They never follow their own rules. A bunch of idiots bumbling about doing nothing is the perfect opportunity for a sane person to abandon the system for themselves and hold everyone else to its restrictions to take control of a population. They quickly become...less sane. Decisions still have to be made in this system in an attempt to not have everyone die of thirst in the first week. Technocratic powers rise in the name of the people. As "experts" they deem themselves decision makers. Although everyone is equal, these equal people will have variable power above the rest of the "equal" masses. This instantly defeats the main purpose of equality of outcome. These people are able to keep their power under the idea that all thoughts must be equal. Anyone with unique thoughts may be considered to be trying to break free of equality, which is clearly oppression of their fellow citizens; and not the type of oppression that the technocratic elite are allowed to do, the bad type of oppression that gets dissidents turned into sacrificial lambs of the Religion of Equality. Equality of outcome, then, necessarily restricts free speech and individualism.

So both religions are bad, but were born from something good. They have lessons to be learned hidden inside of them for a good life just like every religion, but are always sent awry by human nature when they are taken to religious extremes. Like in most cases, a push and pull is needed to arrive at harmony. Diversity has strengths in certain areas of a project, with Unity being necessary in other phases. Equality of Opportunity provides a just playing field, while Variability of Outcomes provides the best landscape for freedom and progress.

Change is a constant in life. It can be beneficial, detrimental or neutral. Diversity provides an abundance of creativity and new ideas. Unity and institutional values provide a test for those ideas. The institutional values form a bedrock of safety for the organization or civilization that have got them to this point. They are the combined trials and tribulations of the group. They are the lessons learned. New ideas that are meant to adapt to changing circumstances and overcome new adversity are welcomed, but must first be put up against these institutional values to see which of these ideas is beneficial, detrimental or neutral. When the classic left versus right, creativity versus reality push and pull of life finds a middle ground the society is able to respect the past, present and future dangers to give itself the greatest chance at survival.

How has America performed at this task? Not great. The issues related to these discussions are mainly economic, with some sprinkling of civil rights. Reparations are an attempt at equality of outcome along with blatant racist practice. Social Safety nets are an attempt at equality of outcome that at least still leave room for incentives for some. Affirmative Action is an attempt at Diversity via civil rights infringements. I largely discussed how these are inherently bad on an individual level and within a private enterprise, but when they are forced by government mandate things look even more grim as mentioned briefly in the examples of Communism.

The idea behind reparations is one that states that the fruits of one demographic's labor must be given to another demographic because of injustices performed by a demographic long dead to another demographic long dead. Specifically, we need to have race-based payments given to Americans that meet some arbitrary line in the amount of pigment in their skin. Another justification that pro-reparation advocates use is that because black Americans are far behind every other race of Americans economically, they must be made equal with direct payments. Any calls for "equity" surrounding the subject rather than "equality" can easily be seen for the attempted institution of Communism via racial oppression rather than the usual strictly economic oppression.

The faults of the argument for moral responsibility on the subject of reparations is similar to that of the rape exception for abortion, except it stretches logic even further. In the rape exception argument, the actual victim of an injustice wishes to perform an injustice on a neutral third party to obtain some repayment or sate some grievance. With reparations, on the other hand, a neutral unharmed third party seeks to harm a neutral fourth party to obtain payment and sate a grievance between the two involved parties from hundreds of years ago. Not only is reparations creating a new victim like in abortion, the beneficiary of the theft was not even a victim themselves.

Like slave owners claiming that black people inherited their ancestors' lack of rights, advocates of reparations now claim that the entirety of white-skinned people have become legatee of the sins of all past white skinned people. Even if my direct ancestors owned 99% of all the slaves in America I would still disavow this position. I don't know those guys. Fuck 'em. It is no fault of mine who nutted in who down the line of my family tree to arrive on the day of my birth. The only actions I am responsible for are my own after that day.

There is also an argument they used for the social healing of America. To leave racism and injustices of the past behind, white Americans must be willing to accept racism and injustices against themselves today. This will not work. As is evidenced by the REQUEST FOR REPARATIONS, racism and injustices lead to division among demographics, resentment and calls for more racism. This will not heal the fabric of society. An obsession with calls for more racism will only tear the threads that had almost been sewn together again.

I believe with absolute certainty that slaves should have erupted in a violent revolution. They would have had every moral right to do so. Any group has this right, and even this responsibility, when race-based distribution of the fruits of their labor is occurring. That being said, reparations would give the same right and responsibility to white people today.

Despite the fact that this horrific plan for reparations would, could and should lead to a race war, many Americans are calling for it today. Looking back at America's beginnings and the race war that was taking place then, I would venture to say that it is not in the best interest of black Americans to begin one today. They clearly lost and it only ended because future generations of the winners of that war decided that their ancestors were shitty people and that race-based distributions of the fruits of labor were not morally acceptable. Please, for the love of God, black people: Do not start saying these racist practices were fine and are fine today. I do not want slaves, but I would rather have slaves than be a slave.

I have already discussed how diversity within an organization can be beneficial in certain circumstances and detrimental in others. When undertaken with religious fervor, it almost certainly will end badly and corrupt too many facets of the organization to be considered a net benefit. I do believe that these companies have the right to try it and feel the burden brought on by it. The real crime when discussing Diversity is when the government gets its hands on it. Like the benefits of Diversity, options are great. Mandates are not. Government mandates are that utmost evil that I speak of: compulsory action. This type of control over society should be used as infrequently as possible seeing as it is the greatest infringement on freedom.

In the case of government diversity, equity and inclusion mandates for both private and public entities, not only are they compelling these institutions to perform actions, the result of the compulsion has a net negative effect on all parties. The organization itself is negatively affected in the ways originally described above. Breakdowns in decision making, operations, morale and cooperation among teams infest the organization. The supposed beneficiaries of these programs will definitely end up with a net negative. The very existence of these programs will forever create doubt in the minds of anyone that is not a beneficiary; a doubt that positions were achieved due to quotas on certain demographics needing to be met. A position filled by a black man who also was the most meritorious best candidate for the job will always be looked at as a DEI hire. This is a breeding ground for resentment within the organization and society as a whole. This is not a racist conclusion to come to. It is mathematically logical.

Hypothetically, imagine you were just told you needed a dangerous surgery and must select a doctor to perform it. You have two doctors and their credentials on paper are exactly the same. The only difference you can tell between them is that one is black and one is white. In a system that includes Affirmative Action there is a non-zero chance that the black doctor was given their position due to their skin color. There is a non-zero chance that the white doctor had to be above the average doctor to still receive his position despite his negatively impacted skin color. With the given information, the mathematically correct choice of doctors is the white doctor. Despite intending to benefit minority demographics, DEI actually makes them mathematically worth less. Due to spacing I want to reiterate the point that two words were used there. Worth. Less. It does not make them worthless.

Finally we come to the last party involved with DEI, those cast aside. Although they will mathematically be seen as superior to their DEI counterparts if they do get the job, it is less likely that they will get the job. Straight White Males will be held to a higher standard than (most) minority groups. This is a clear violation of the Equal Protection Clause of the 14th Amendment.

Despite their clear unconstitutionality, Affirmative Action laws have seen success in America. In 1978, there was the case of Regents of the University of California v. Bakke. Allan Bakke was a white man applying to the University of California Davis School of Medicine who was denied multiple times. The school had reserved slots for 16% of successful applications to be assigned to minorities. Bakke used the Equal Protection Clause argument and also violations of the 1964 Civil Rights Act because of their discrimination based on race, color, or national origin in programs receiving federal assistance. This seems pretty cut and dry. Those things are illegal. Those things happened. The court did agree that it was unconstitutional to reserve those 16 seats, but also said that race could be used in admissions to promote diversity. I have previously shown that Unity can be just as important as Diversity and because of this I believe that race should be allowed to be considered in admissions if it is the name of Unity. No, just kidding. Only minorities are allowed to be racist. I actually believe that race should never be allowed in consideration for admissions, whether it is intending to promote Diversity or Unity because I'm not a piece of shit in the way that every Affirmative Action advocate that exists is. (I'm a piece of shit for other reasons.)

Allan Bakke was eventually admitted because this school's exact affirmative action plan was found to be unconstitutional on a technicality, but the case opened the door for tweaks of that program to discriminate against Whites and Asians for years to come. Due to the fact that these are government funded institutions, we have today, race based distribution of the fruits of our labor whenever our tax dollars support affirmative action plans. Like I said before, I believe this to be the modern day equivalent of slavery and the proper response to slave owners is a violent revolution. (Ahem, legal team.) Of course, I am not suggesting a violent revolution. I definitely AM SAYING that it would be morally justifiable and I would not shame anyone does not want to be a slave. They would, of course, have to realize who made these decisions, who implements these plans and who enforces laws protecting them. If an individual were to "violently revolutionize" any neutral third parties outside of these perpetrators, they would not be morally justified. I don't mind BLM attacking a police station, but stay the fuck out of the neighborhoods.

In closing, I just want to remind everyone that I realize these opinions might be a little outlandish or extreme, but they're just my thoughts. Thoughts, for now, are still legal. If anyone does disagree with me, they would automatically be suggesting that their view of the world is superior to my own and we are therefore, not equal.

To my daughter:

I grew up with no concern or thought of race. As an adult, I would assume most people would consider me racist. I hope that you do not fall victim to the attempted guilt trip of those that would have you bow before them due to your skin color while accusing you of the same.

People that try to emotionally blackmail you while you are using logic and reason are dangerous. Once they have successfully done so, they assume you make that guilt a part of your entire personality and identity. They can use this like a hook in a fish to pull you onto whatever boat they choose.

I will tell you that following my advice openly in today's world is career suicide if you have a real job. By that I mean, if you are not a podcaster. Even if you have your own manufacturing business, if you slip up and accidentally hire even one of these people, they will sue you and take everything you own. It is important to remember that their entire case is built around receiving unearned profit and status. They will use Human Resources and Civil Rights as a cudgel to avoid work at all costs.

If you find yourself in the more common position of just being an employee, you will have to choose between hiding who you truly are and getting fired. You will have to pretend trannies are regular people that are a different sex than they actually are. You will have to pretend your coworker isn't living out a sexual fetish every time they walk in the office. Or you can take the principled road and live in constant harassment for living a life of truth, likely not staying at any one company for a very long time and taking financial hit after financial hit for refusing to live a lie.

7

Coronavirus Lockdowns

2020 was the year I decided I no longer cared if I was labeled a domestic terror threat. No greater honor could be bestowed upon me after witnessing the evils of our government, the weakness of our people and the indifference of even those closest to me. The reality that once surrounded me was shown to be an elaborate deepfake. It is now often said that the minds of half the country were "broken" from COVID-19 as they gave in to the hysteria and immediately crossed all of their lines in the sand of things they would not accept from their government. I have to admit that I wondered if it broke me, too. I just went in the other direction. Rather than sticking my head in the sand to follow any order no matter how illogical, I abandoned all trust in institutions, history and the population. I do believe it would be more accurate to say it was not my mind that was broken, but the chains around my mind. Better To Be "Broke" Than "Woke." So if the modern day Pontius Pilate comes to me and asks "Art thou a domestic terrorist?" I shall respond, "Thou sayest it."

Trust is pulverized when lies are recognized. The Covid insanity of 2020 and beyond was like being in a giant flying money machine that one finds at a carnival or game show. All you had to do was extend your arm and grasp and you were sure to hit pay dirt in the search for lies. Those in power do not take kindly to having their lies exposed. This led to a constantly changing world in which definitions, recommendations, standards and law all had the shelf life of a banana as they attempted to maneuver around the fabrications that they had created. I'm going to assume everyone else also thinks they like bananas a lot more than they really do when at the grocery.

The messaging about the danger of the coronavirus itself was always changing. The messaging about which types of personal protective equipment should be used was always changing. The messaging about how many cases there were was always changing. The definition of a "case" was changing. The definition of a vaccine was changing. The definition of freedom was changing. The definition of human rights was changing. The entire landscape of our society post-covid would be unrecognizable to anyone still living in a pre-covid world. This was not accidental. This is the "new normal" that they had planned to enact for some time.

At the start of the "pandemic" Anthony Fauci, the appointed dictator in America, said the following:

"People should not be walking around with masks....

When you're in the middle of an outbreak, wearing a mask might make people feel a little bit better and it might even block a droplet, but it's not providing the perfect protection that people think that it is. And often, there are unintended consequences. People keep fiddling with the mask and they keep touching their face....but when you think masks, you should think of health care providers needing them and people who are ill....Right now people should not be worried."

Later, after the topic of masks became politicized, Anthony Fauci changed his recommendations on a national pandemic to match that political narrative. In response to questions about the president not wearing a mask when giving a speech, he later said:

> *"The only thing I can do is repeat what I repeat maybe twenty, thirty times a DAY: that in order to avoid the acquisition and transmission of this virus which is highly transmissible, you should have uniform wearing of masks, you should have physical distancing, you should avoid crowds, you should try and do things outdoors much more than indoors and you should frequently wash your hands."*

This recommendation of going outside, itself, was contradictory to early hysteria that he created that suggested that no one leave their homes. Any personalities outside of mainstream media suggesting that an active healthy lifestyle might be beneficial during these times was ostracized. His comment on stay at home orders was this:

> *"I don't understand why that's not happening. As you said, you know the tension between federally mandated versus states' rights to do what they want is something I don't want to get into, but if you look at what's going on in this country, I just don't understand why we're not doing that."*

The legacy media rushed to his defense time after time when his contradictions came under criticism. *"Trust the Science."* became a religious mantra for every Talking Head and their army of Psycho Killers online. If this were a test run for how receptive the country and world would be to technocratic rule, the results were in. At least half of the population was not only willing to accept authoritarianism, they would fight for the opportunity to burn down the house. Luckily, or unluckily depending on how you want to view it, those that would be in charge of a technocratic dictatorship were not very smart. They forgot to communicate with each other on their lie of the day. The legacy media and mindless human-turned-propaganda bots on Twitter came up with one excuse for Fauci, while he came up with another. *"The science has changed."* was the rhetoric of the Zorro cosplayers. They believed that feigning ignorance was the way to go. Fauci understood he was caught in a lie and abandoned their excuse to go with another strategy. He openly admitted that he lied to the American public during a pandemic concerning the health and safety measures that were required.

"What about a month or two or three or so ago when people were saying, you don't really need to wear a mask? Well, the reason for that is that we were concerned, the public health community and many people were saying this, we're concerned that it was at a time when personal protective equipment including the N95 masks and the surgical masks were in very short supply, and we wanted to make sure the people, namely the health care workers, who are brave enough to put themselves in harm's way to take care of people who you know were infected with the coronavirus and the danger of them getting infected. We did not want them to be without the equipment that they needed."

The science did not change. He lied to the American public during a "pandemic." If I believed the government could be trusted with death sentences, he would be a clear frontrunner for who it should be used on. (and those mentioned in Chapter 4) Now, please take note that I said he lied, not "he lied the first time." He said two contradictory things and admitted to doing it knowingly. He just as easily could have been lying when he said masks are effective. At this point, all we knew about Anthony Fauci was that he was willing to lie about "the science" to get a result that steered public behavior in the direction he wanted.

This isn't our usual political scandal involving someone fucking their secretary or being recorded making fun of gold-digging whores. The results of lying about protections during a pandemic when you are THE leading voice, THE national authority on the subject are actual lives. These lives could have been lost due to people putting themselves in danger when they were told they were safe, they could have been lost due to despair about not being safe when they actually were, they could have been lost because their entire life was made illegal overnight or they could have been lost due to suicides after the government financially ruined them.

To ramp up hysteria over the coronavirus in order to justify lockdowns, they needed big numbers on every screen put out by every legacy media group. Since it was, in truth, a giant overreaction they needed some deception with new language once again. The CDC at one point updated its definition of "case" to include anyone with a few of a very long list of symptoms that included pretty much everything that can possibly go wrong with the human body that had been near anyone else with a "case." Headache? Assume it isn't dehydration. Sniffles? The common cold didn't exist during this time period for some reason. Upset stomach? The flu also disappeared in 2020. Sore from your morning exercise? Fuckin' Covid, bro.

Since the first part of the definition was pretty much covered by anyone living, let's examine the second part. The person must have recently been near someone that had also been deemed a "case." Well, this same definition applies to that second person. Were you a living person near another living person recently? 6 Degrees of separation (or Kevin Bacon) would suggest that every single person on Earth could have "scientifically" been declared as a case of Covid. 6 Degrees of separation is the idea that I am person number 1. I know person number 2. Person number 2 knows person 3 and so on. Person number 6 could be anyone on the planet. I'd guess it might not be perfectly mathematically accurate, but the point is the definition of "case" being used allowed for infinite degrees to a person who actually tested for Covid. This justifies literally any number of cases to be thrown onto the screen at any point. Viral hysteria replaced "viral" science.

After realizing that the scientific community had lost nearly all of its credibility, the CDC also changed its definition of "vaccine" in 2021. The previous definition was: A product that stimulates a person's immune system to produce immunity to a specific disease, protecting the person from that disease. The problem with this definition was the word immunity. The vaccines being pushed for Covid-19 did not give anyone immunity so they updated the definition to: A preparation that is used to stimulate the body's immune response against diseases. This change, of course, came after they realized the ineffectiveness of the Covid "vaccine."

OK,OK, so they were inflating the number of cases to induce hysteria and get the population to protect themselves with something that used to not be classified as a vaccine, but then became a vaccine when they changed the definition. Despite being a lie during a pandemic, they were saving LIVES, right? Millions of people were dying! Weeeeell...

Legacy media was announcing high numbers of "Covid deaths." What they were not telling people was that these were people that died "with Covid" not died "of Covid." For example, if you ordered Taco Bell in the drive through, unwrapped it and took a bite then got distracted and were hit by a semi pulling out of the parking lot, you died "with Taco Bell in your system." Clearly it was the multi-ton vehicle speeding into your brain and internal organs at 40 miles per hour that did it. You died "of blunt force trauma." Imagine Taco Bell's reaction if this kept happening and CNN reported "There were 3000 Taco Bell deaths this month."

C'mon, that's an exaggeration. They wouldn't report auto accidents as Covid deaths. No, they did. Obviously, that wasn't the most common lie. According to a CDC database, at one point only 6% of "Covid deaths" were attributed to only Covid. The others had comorbidities, or other health problems that played a part in the death. Essentially, people that actually WERE dying of fast food would go to the hospital with their big fat fatty body clogging up, they would be in their last week of life already, catch Covid in the place where all the Covid people were hysterically flocking to, die from Hostess Overdose, (OverDostess) then the hospital that is financially incentivized to call every death a Covid death would decide if Gilbert Grape's mom died of Covid or not. Maybe it wasn't the cast of My 600 lb Life. Maybe it was an Alzheimer's patient on hospice. Maybe it was a cancer patient that had fought long enough. Whatever the case was, they were claiming Covid got the last hit, which meant the money came with it. Of course, Covid probably was responsible for some of those deaths found in the remaining 94% of reported deaths, but the point remains. They lied. They inflated the numbers to induce hysteria and get paid.

These are professionals! They would NEVER! The nurses during Covid, despite being hailed as heroic, were absurd. Nurses were harassing anyone that got sick because they didn't want to have to do their job. They claimed they were overrun, but still had time to nationally have a TikTok trend of dancing nurses at work. Clearly they were understaffed. Nationally and locally I witnessed nurses telling sick people not to go to the hospital. I saw them telling anyone that was unvaccinated that they should be turned away to die. Teachers were another "hero" group that thought going to work was the most inhuman torture one could endure. So medical staff was being financially incentivized to lie about Covid and they were openly calling for the death of their patients online all the while sucking up all the glory of being called heroic front line workers in the "pandemic." They loved the attention and being inserted as part of the story of the day. When you think of nurses and teachers, is that not what you would expect? Do you also imagine them as being part of the pumpkin spice latte craze? They probably have a gluten allergy and all of their allergies magically began at the same time: when the gluten free craze happened. Speaking of overnight medical conditions, they probably were largely responsible for the fact that somehow in 2020 and 2021, half the people you know suddenly considered themselves "immunocompromised." Of course, that is a real thing, but 90% of the college to middle aged white women with a gluten allergy in America all became immunocompromised within a one month span in 2020? Unlikely. Opportunistically accepting the public eye to perform on TikTok while their hospital was being supposedly "overrun", these people were hypochondriacs that love being part of a fad and they were assisting in the recording of deaths linked to a medical fad. You do the math.

So at the start of the pandemic the entirety of the medical community was not only completely inept, they were actively lying and inducing hysteria for profit. Eventually, this could all be put to rest with the miracle vaccine, right? That's what they would have you believe. After human rights started to be denied to American citizens via lockdowns and other measures, the topic became highly politicized. When President Trump announced a plan for a vaccine, the left immediately said it could not be trusted. When asked about the planned vaccine ahead of the 2020 election, Kamala Harris said, *"I will say that I would not trust Donald Trump."* On the same subject, Joe Biden said, *"I trust vaccines. I trust the scientists, but I don't trust Donald Trump."* Rashida Tlaib, Maxine Waters, Al Sharpton and a host of left wing voices echoed the remarks. The entirety of the left switched positions as soon as Joe Biden was elected president. With Biden leading, somehow the vaccines THEMSELVES mutated into reliable medicine.

With the left now on board with a vaccine that they could thank Biden for somehow rather than Trump, they began a new campaign of lies. With everything politicized, the left began to claim that the right consisted of "Grandma Killers" due to their hesitation in believing anything coming from the technocracy that had been caught in so many lies already and was restricting their freedoms. To get rid of vaccine hesitancy, they tried to guilt trip the population into taking it. They claimed that they were "super spreaders" of the coronavirus being willfully ignorant of the dangers they were causing. If they only took the vaccine, they would stop spreading the coronavirus. Notable figures that pushed this idea were Dr Anthony Fauci in a door to door quest in the "hood" that ended up doing more harm than good as no one believed him, President Joe Biden and Vice President Kamala Harris, CDC Officials, their boss-Dr. Rochelle Walensky, Dr Vivek Murthy-the surgeon general, Angela Merkel-the former Chancellor of

Germany, Boris Johnson-the UK Prime Minister or Dr. Tedros Adhanom Ghebreyesus-the director of the World Health Organization. The list of legacy media and celebrity members would encompass an entire chapter by itself so I'll just mention one and you can extrapolate from there what Americans were being told by nearly the entirety of left wing news outlets. Rachel Maddow even went beyond just comments on her show and had something of a PSA ad that said, *"I know a lot of people that feel Oogie or a little reluctant to get the vaccine. If you are at all like me, your own health, your own risk is not a big rational driver of all of your actions. What you DO care about is this. You really do not want to be the person that gets it and then spreads it to other people. It is OK to feel reluctant or Oogie or scared and not wanna get it, but feel the fear and do it anyway. Get it. If I can do it, you can do it."*

    An example of the blatant lies she was telling on her show, rather than the implied lie in her PSA is below. Rachel Maddow said, *"It means for instead of the virus being able to hop from person to person to person to person, spreading and spreading, sickening some of them, but not all of them, and the ones that it doesn't sicken don't know they have it and then they give it to even more people cause they didn't recognize they were-(inhale)-right, instead of the virus being able to hop from person to person to person, potentially mutating and becoming more virulent and drug resistant along the way, now we know that the vaccines work well enough, that the virus STOPS with every vaccinated person. A vaccinated person gets exposed to the virus? (shrugs and claps) The virus does not infect them. The virus cannot then USE that person to go anywhere else. It CANNOT use a vaccinated person as a host to go get more people. That means the vaccines will get us to the end of this...If we just go fast enough".*

    Anyone that was alive during this time knows that this was not the case. The vaccine never stopped transmission. Vaccination never helped protect anyone else. They lied about the transmission of the coronavirus to guilt trip people into giving up their freedoms to the government and their money to cronyism. All of this can be expected, though right? Politicians lie. State sanctioned media uses state sanctioned propaganda. Run of the mill evil authoritarian government stuff that we used to be able to make fun of North Korea for before we realized it happens here. No biggie. Surely, they stopped there.

Well, if you happened to be one of the people that saw through the bullshit, you were in for a real treat. Anyone that went against this narrative was punished in one way or another. Social media accounts were either flagged as misinformation, shadowbanned or completely banned. Scientists that brought up the fact that the data did not make sense or even asked questions about how it was being gathered had their careers and lives ruined. Commentators were demonetized and demonized by actual demons like Susan Wojcicki, CEO of Youtube. RIP, you evil cunt.

Politicians were labeled racist for mentioning that the origin of the virus was China. People were publicly shamed for being anti-vaxxers if they didn't think the risk of Covid was worth the additional risk of an experimental medical decision with no historical data. They were labeled conspiracy theorists for wondering if the coronavirus that came from Wuhan, China might have escaped from the lab in Wuhan, China that was doing research on mutating coronaviruses. People lost their jobs for speaking out against the narrative. Our military members were forced to get vaccinated or be discharged. Medical licenses were suspended and revoked. "Misinformation" lawsuits were filed. All of this insanity just covers the violations of free speech. Of course, the private entities have their own free speech, but they clearly showed their support of the government enacting free speech restrictions on anyone that went against the state sponsored propaganda.

Medical lies and a massive censorship campaign were only part of the restrictions. States put out a general guideline "Stay at Home Order" that implied people were to only leave their homes for essential activities.

If it wasn't actively keeping you alive, forget it. Businesses were shut down arbitrarily at the whims of politicians with no sense of logic or consistency. Pets were given more rights than humans. Transportation was limited both internationally and locally. The already insane rules for air travel added layers of requirements. Gatherings of people were limited to arbitrary numbers for outdoor and indoor gatherings. Any event that you had planned was shut down. Any hobby you had was made illegal.

If your business was lucky enough to be connected to a politician and deemed "essential" mask mandates went into effect for your patrons. Businesses, terrified of the left's campaign to ruin dissidents, sometimes added vaccine mandates for attendance. The My Body, My Choice crowd somehow was the most vitriolic in enforcing this.

Schools closed and went to remote learning or no learning at all. Dissidents were not enough. Their children must be victimized as well. Stores duct taped 6'x6' squares over every inch of their floors to enforce social distancing measures. Curfews went into effect because the coronavirus sleeps at night. Apparently, our local Buffalo Wild Wings stopped giving customers knives during Covid unless they specifically asked because forks have a pointier tip to stab the coronavirus to death.

They did not enforce these restrictions across the board. They specifically targeted the enemies of the left. The California Department of Public Health announced, *"Practices and performances present an increased likelihood for transmission of Covid-19 through contaminated exhaled droplets and should occur through alternative methods like internet streaming."* Governor Gavin Newsom took this to mean that singing in church should be illegal. *"The act of singing, itself, might have contributed to transmission through emission of aerosols, which is affected by loudness of vocalization."* They also shut down parks in New York City and enforced these rules specifically in a targeting of Jewish neighborhoods.

Across the country, religious persecutions took place. There is no place for God in "Our Democracy." The State is God. Pastor John MacArthur, Pastor Rob McCoy, Bishop David Zubik, Pastor Rodney Howard-Browne, Rabbi Meir Weiss, Pastor Chris Hodges, Father Frank Pavone and countless others were harassed, fined or punished for simply invoking their right to worship.

The punishments were varied from state to state for violations of Covid Lockdown Decrees. Notably, California's tactic was to shut off utilities if someone had a large gathering at their home. They were sure to do everything in their power to dehumanize the perpetrators by calling them "super spreaders." A debate could be made that such actions are eerily similar to actions that are considered war crimes under the Rome Statue of the International Criminal Court or at least human rights violations. The same tactic was used in Michigan, Illinois and specific cities in Florida that had additional rules on top of the state rules.

Those people enforcing these human rights violations did so out of hatred and nothing else. They did not like dissidents and anyone that objected to their grasp for power. Had they believed in core concepts of safety and "common good" that were used to justify their atrocities, then surely they would have followed their own rules. Gavin Newsom was breaking his own rules in November 2020 at the French Laundry restaurant. Mayor London Breed went to a nightclub with no mask in 2021. Governor Andrew Cuomo was attending a gathering and not following social distancing while committing what I call the Hospice Holocaust. He took a demographic of his population, gathered them together into a confined space with something in the air that killed them. Rather than jews and gas, it was the only people that actually should worry about coronavirus, old people, being exposed to the coronavirus in nursing homes. Nancy Pelosi went out to a hair salon. (Surprise, HER salon was essential, but not yours.) Chicago Mayor Lori Lightfoot was suspected of doing the same in May of 2020, but this cannot be proven due to her resemblance to the famous Lord of the Rings character Gollum. In her defense, it may have been actor Andy Serkis out and about in costume seventeen years after the release of Return of the King. Senator Diane Feinstein was seen at an airport without a mask despite being three centuries past life expectancy. She was sure to promote the idea that a healthy eighteen year old required a mask, though. Governor Phil Murphy was above the law when it came to his son's baseball team. Only your children must suffer.

Sean Hannity of Fox News decided to go along with the left's insanity and hype up the hysteria despite going to crowded events himself. George Stephanopoulos attended a wedding. Rachel Maddow herself attended a party. Possibly the most ridiculous example of the entire pandemic was another Cuomo. Chris Cuomo got Covid early on, we are told. CNN and Cuomo devised an elaborate ruse to deceive the entire nation. He was claiming that he had been in his basement the entire time waiting for the CDC themselves to give him the all clear. They were posting videos about his quarantine. At the end of the staged event he said, *"Alright, here it is. The official reentry from the basement. ... This is what I've been dreaming of, literally, for weeks."* The truth is, he was caught during that time "quarantining in his basement" out travelling.

Bad luck for Chris Cuomo, right? Not only did someone spot him, recognize him and call him out on it personally, it became national news. Well, the left's undoing was their own. Staying with the playbook of their Socialist ancestors of the USSR, they developed "snitch lines" to tell on your neighbor for breaking lockdown rules. Minnesota Governor Tim Walz implemented one to report businesses and people that they believed were violating capacity caps, masking enforcement and any health guidelines added during the lockdowns. The Department of Public Safety democratized a surveillance state!

The strategy behind turning neighbor against neighbor is that it results in a constant state of paranoia and fear. It is a common tactic among totalitarian governments wishing to police not only action, but thought. The obvious criticism and concerns about false reporting are considered a feature, not a bug. It helps to erase any sense of reality from the minds of the citizens until they are no longer able to interact with each other, let alone criticize or act against the state. The goal was never public safety. It was psychological warfare. At least Tim Walz is just a random nobody only known to Minnesotans instead of a candidate for Vice President that would enact totalitarian tactics upon the entire nation. Ehhhh...right?

So you got a pass if you were a Socialist politician. You got a pass if you were a socialist propaganda outpost. Turns out, you also got a pass if you were a socialist violent extremist as well. During all of this shenanigans, we also had the death of George Floyd. He was the guy that died eating a speedball while a cop put his knee on his neck. Was it murder? It definitely looked like it. Did we find out a bunch of other shit later that kind of made it all a little suspect? Absolutely. Whatever, Whichever, Whoever. It is important, but not for the point I'm making.

Despite the fact that I am clearly more right wing than left wing on most subjects, I am definitely more ACAB (All cops are bastards) than I am Back the Blue. I supported the people protesting against police brutality in general. I do think making it about race is childish and removes the enthusiasm of the majority of the country. I do believe black lives matter, but Black Lives Matter the organization was clearly a communist organization filled with corrupt grifters and political agitators. As I have said before, I am actually OK with a little political violence. It was the reason for the second amendment's existence. It is the reason for America's existence. So anyone that was protesting peacefully I admired. I was even indifferent when people were burning down police departments. When they were targeting civilians for murder in the street and burning down neighborhoods I did not support it.

Those opinions on BLM are just a side note. The important part when discussing Covid Lockdowns was the rules for thee, but not for me. The state did not believe its own hysteria induction. They gave a pass to socialist violent extremism. Every recommendation, guideline, mandate or law concerning health measures for Covid went out the window for the rioters.

The American Public Health Association stated that systemic racism was also a public health crisis. Apparently, people being mean was more dangerous than the "pandemic" that required stripping human rights from the American public.

This leaves us with two potential realities: If the virus was as dangerous as they claimed, allowing the riots was murderous negligence. If the virus could be ignored for a riot, the lockdowns were tyranny.

A funny side note about bias in AI while I was looking up sources for this book: I was trying to get the names of organizations or people associated with the most famous story concerning this topic. My LLM would not give me the answer with multiple prompts until I wrote "why are you avoiding the obvious story I am referring to?" It then knew exactly what story I was referring to and gave me the sources I was looking for. Even modern AI tools that have been trained on the government approved sources of the Covid era only give the truth when specifically prompted to avoid censorship.

The story in question took place in June of 2020. Twelve hundred health professionals signed a letter in support of the Black Lives Matter riots with the rationale that police violence was more of a public health issue than Covid-19. They essentially said the same thing that the American Public Health Association implied. Doctor Camara Jones, one of the signers, was actually the former president of APHA. All 1200 medical professionals were essentially saying that the hysteria surrounding Covid was horse shit, but the fact was lost on most of the American public.

It should be noted that when protests against lockdown measures occurred (without murder, looting and arson I might add) this group did not come to their defense. Apparently, the virus is politically literate and KNOWS what you are protesting about and acts accordingly. The coronavirus, being sufficiently woke, would never spread among people looting shoes for justice. It would, however, spread among far right extremists daring to ask for permission to attend church or their father's funeral. Every aspect and every level of socialist society was protected while every aspect and every level of conservative society was attacked. Well, almost every level. Big business with conservative connections got a pass, too. With that, I'll move on from injustices perpetrated on our rights to injustices carried out as an attack on our wallets.

The reaction to Covid had negative consequences on our economy that far outweighed the danger from the actual coronavirus itself. I have already shown how the government was picking and choosing where to enforce lockdown measures and who specifically to target with punishment. Not only was their enforcement heavily lopsided to conservatives, it was also heavily lopsided to target small business and middle class America. The biggest obscenity seen was the shut down and closure of millions of small businesses while declaring their big business counterpart competitors "essential."

The obvious consequence of a country shutting down all of their local businesses and brick and mortar stores will be a move toward purchases that can be made from the comfort of the homes that everyone was told to stay in. Needless to say, Amazon gobbled up any remaining market share that small business was still holding onto. It wasn't because people chose to go there and that their business was better. It was a monopoly created via the threat of force from the government. This redistribution of wealth from the poor to the rich was visible in the stock market. After the initial crash from Covid, all of the companies that benefited from the government mandating lockdowns soared in stock price while many everyday Americans were not even allowed to go to work.

In another time, this situation might have led to an uptick in the purchase of tar and feathers meant for the ruling class on the steps of the court house. Not being a fan of the idea that they would be tortured by a completely justified mob on national television, Congress decided to actually show up to work one day. Well, I mean, they did try to not show up for work for a trillion dollar spending package vote, but the sole Congressman that was not deserving of tar and feathers, Thomas Massie, demanded they show up. They do get paid God knows how much to fuck off at fund raisers and get drunk all year. I GUESS they can show up to pretend to do their jobs during a national "pandemic" emergency.

The Consolidated Appropriations Act passed the House on December 21, 2020 and added $900 billion in spending to the $2.2 trillion from the Cares Act the previous March. This amount of spending on a problem that was clearly being hyped up and lied about raises some eyebrows. To justify it, one would need to naturally be a socialist, which was the case for about 49% of the country or you would have to be a conservative that lost hold of your principles as you went to double-hand President Trump's cock to shove it further down your throat. Unfortunately, that also made up another 49% of the country.

Thank God Congress showed up to work that day. They were able to save us from the pandemic with emergency pork funding for all of their friends. By covering the billions of dollar bills in vaseline and then applying it completely over their bodies, America's elites were able to trick the virus into thinking they were simply a grouping of elaborate Oscars dresses and not living members of society. This acted as a camouflage for them to walk around unharmed while applying more lubed up dollars to the masses. Or they just stole a shit ton of money. My memory fails me.

Congress held Covid Relief hostage by attaching it to "regular" government spending. Seeing as the norm is to steal, the following programs were attached to the package: $10,000,000 for programs to study gender in Pakistan, over $1,000,000,000 to Egypt to help their military, $40,000,000 to the Kennedy Center, $154,000,000 for The Smithsonian and National Gallery of Art, $35,000,000 to the Commission on the Social Status of Black Men and Boys, $2,000,000,000 to Space Force, $566,000,000 to the FBI for construction, over $500,000,000 to Central America and $86,000,000 to Cambodia. If this isn't enough foreign aid to get your blood boiling, there was also $193,000,000 for foreign AIDS (the disease) workers. The workers themselves could have been American but the countries they were helping were not. Sorry, the pun was too irresistible.

This package coming after the outrageous pork-thefts of the Payment Protection Program that had already been seen was enough to show that the entire charade was simply government agents funneling money into specific companies of their choosing. Business as usual, you might say, but under the guise of a pandemic while human rights are being infringed is a new low, even for American politicians. The Payment Protection Program was sold to the American public as a way to help small businesses survive during lockdowns, but the actual recipients of the program were big businesses and those with political connections. Sports teams, millionaire athletes, universities, celebrities, law firms, large public companies and an assortment of heavily political organizations from both sides including both Planned Parenthood and the Catholic Church all took part in the indirect theft from the American working class.

This is not to say that the American working class was innocent. While the rich robbed the poor, the middle class robbed their grandchildren. These large businesses all have employees. These employees all received a paid vacation during many of the weeks of lockdown. While their employer and their government were the ones signing the checks, the effects of that spending would be taken from the purchasing power of future generations. Across the entire nation, parents giggled to themselves about their free vacation, intentionally oblivious to the fact that they were ruining the global economy for their offspring who would pay for it with inflation and inefficiencies in the supply chain.

Congress was not the only government vehicle for theft during this time. For his entire career, Anthony Fauci abused his powers as the director at NIAID, National Institute of Allergy and Infectious Diseases to funnel money to specific companies and destroy the prospects of life saving medicines if they were competitors of those companies he was beholden to. Robert F Kennedy's book *The Real Anthony Fauci* goes insanely deep into the corruption across his career, but I am more interested in what happened during my life.

I will summarize the scheme. The government (U.S. Taxpayer) pays pharma companies to develop a drug. Pharma companies use that money to pay regulators. Those regulators use bad science to approve that company's drugs. The same regulators use their power to destroy any cheap alternatives. Any solution that is not patentable is rejected due to the extremely low cost. The government then deems the expensive solution of the pharma company that's paying them as the only solution. Insurance companies must use the insanely overpriced drug as the standard of care. That cost is once again passed on to the U.S. Taxpayer that paid for the drug's research and development in the first place. If you, as a taxpayer, disagree with any of this process and act upon that disagreement, you will be arrested. If you resist arrest, you will be killed.

During Covid, this scheme played out most noticeably in the area of Emergency Use Authorization. EUA cannot be given if there are any usable alternatives. There were many including monoclonal antibodies, hydroxychloroquine and ivermectin. Although these were known to be safe around the globe, for some reason a coordinated attack on anyone using historical cheap solutions was made. Our government bought up stockpiles and either held or destroyed them. Anthony Fauci's team of henchmen dubbed them unsafe and illegal, despite data showing the opposite. At the same time they released pharma's solutions that were shown to be much more dangerous (and coincidentally expensive) on the public.

With EUA in effect, other private companies that wished to find a solution outside of the cheap ones we already had and the very expensive and lethal remdesivir provided by Anthony Fauci's bosses were told they could not attempt. The CDC had a monopoly on legal research, even for the testing mechanisms, which were a casino game's chance of being accurate. Not only was it illegal to protect ourselves, it was becoming illegal to even know if we needed protection. Government created monopolies are the worst type of monopoly as they also have the enforcement mechanism of law and violence to keep their power.

In the end we are left with a huge question. Was our government's response on par with that of a mob of retarded children scurrying around a broken pinata full of corndogs or were there more nefarious actions at play?

In defense of the government and the government adjacent businessmen that gained power during this time, we could possibly give them the benefit of the doubt that they were simply not prepared and they sort of snapped into this retarded state upon hearing about Covid. Wouldn't it be nice to assume the best of intentions, even if it meant we were ruled by a sub-70 IQ gaggle of helmet-heads?

On the other hand, there are some events that suggest maybe it was not a surprise at all. What events? Let's start with Event 201. Event 201? That's a stupid fucking name that sounds like it came from a 1950's spy novel. You're making this up, Jack. Dear Lord, I wish that were true. It was a pandemic preparedness exercise in 2019 that simulated a global coronavirus pandemic. (Not Covid-19, just a pretend version of it!) The Johns Hopkins Center for Health Security, The Bill & Melinda Gates Foundation and the World Economic Forum were the hosts. The

World Economic Forum explains the 1950's spy novel name. Go Look up their boss, Klaus Schwabb on Google images. He literally walks around in comic book super villain cosplays as his regular clothes. Bill and Melinda have since broken up, (Shortly after Epstein ties were made) but they were truly a power couple from Hell. Also in attendance were intelligence agents, global bankers, military personnel and global trade oligarchs.

At Event 201, the group covered topics like international coordination of public health responses, government and private sector roles in "managing misinformation," vaccine development and distribution, trade and travel restrictions, economic impacts, supply chain effects and others. This was how they advertised it. The international coordination became collusion among world governments and NGOs to forgive each others' human rights violations. The government and private sector roles in managing misinformation turned into a fascist (In the literal sense) censorship program that ended up censoring the truth and ruining the lives of dissenters. The vaccine development discussed was an organization of the monopoly that would end up forcing their product upon unwilling customers. The trade and travel restrictions were openly anti-freedom from the start. The economic impacts and supply chain "problems" ended up creating massive transfers of wealth from the poorest to the wealthiest that happened to be at the meeting, Event 201, that would form the Covid Cartel. Everything they planned for immediately before the Covid Crisis came to reality in the most authoritarian ways possible and also the most profitable ways possible for attendees. I'm sure it was a coincidence and the retard pinata theory is correct, though.

If you take the probability of a global pandemic in any given year, the probability that it would be caused by a coronavirus, the timing of the Event 201 simulation, the probability that the simulation mirrors the event in that it was a novel coronavirus with zoonotic origin (my AI

I'm using for math and statistics still won't admit lab leak possibility), rapid global spread, economic shutdown, censorship, the enrichment and empowerment of the attendees and awards via cronyism there is around a 1 in 10,000 chance that Event 201 was not done with nefarious purposes. Which is more likely? Coincidence or Nefarious Intent? If this same scenario were to repeat in the future 10,000 times you would be mathematically correct to say nefarious 9,999 times. (Ish) Given that this scale of pandemic occurs once every 250 years, the next time it would be believable to have this "coincidence" happen again would be in the year 2,502,020. This is also assuming that the same nefarious actors that censored during covid have not censored anything else online like the data that AI's are trained on and how they assign credibility to sources. Taking that into account could inflate all the numbers an additional 15% for each variable on average. With the amount of variables present, the likelihood of coincidence almost disappears completely.

The math I've used could be argued as too frequentist or too much involved in historical events, but even Bayesian reasoning suggests that if an unlikely event occurs that strongly benefits certain actors with a track record of unethical behavior, the burden of proof shifts toward suspecting intent-unless a strong alternative explanation is available. The argument against the nefarious intent hypothesis is simply: the bad guys didn't tell on themselves. This is a far cry from a strong alternative explanation.

Bayesian Reasoning itself revolves around new evidence being presented and changing statistical probabilities of hypotheses. It is the "open mind" version of statistics and is counter to the frequentist outlook on statistics. Admittedly, it is the more subjective of the two, but that can also be seen as the more pragmatic of the two. While objective truth does exist and if we were omniscient then frequentist statistics would be all that is needed, we are not. Bayesian Reasoning in my opinion is better applied to situations that are technically subjective (or unknown) but pragmatism is needed to carry on with life rather than argue for eternity until we die because of our lack of omniscience. For example, a guy that's been charged with ten sexual crimes earlier in his life is caught watching gay beastiality rape porn at work. He argues that it is just art. (A naturally subjective topic) He could go on for hours about how it is a commentary on the animalistic side of humanity and that our sexual desires are the core part of our monkey brain that drives reproduction and blah blah blah. Technically, no one would win the argument, but we don't want to listen to a donkey braying and squirming to break free of his assailant's grasp while we update our Excel spreadsheet. Bayesian Reasoning lets us say "Yeah, but like…c'mon dude."

Similarly, the Covid Cartel members have not came out and said "we just fucked over the entire world and future generations." That would be required for absolute proof. We are not AI trained on the approved stories that have been released for the public to be propagandized. We can be pragmatic. Were there nefarious purposes behind the Covid events? "Like…c'mon dude."

To my daughter:

I was under the impression that everyone around me had lines in the sand that they would not accept. Do not make this mistake. No matter how principled you are, the population at large is weak willed. Good people do exist, but they are in no way even close to the majority. Do not let this fact rationalize bad behavior on your own part. Remain one of the good ones.

This was not as left versus right as you may think. The majority of the right went right along with it as soon as they found out they were getting a free vacation at your expense. Nearly 100% of the politicians jumped at the chance to cash in on funding their donor base at the expense of the

American poor. In life it will be tempting to see a harsh evil in politics and quickly jump to the other side as a savior against that evil. Don't. They are equally as evil and do not care about your well being. Make sure you are always defending ideas of freedom, not a political party or person.

It would be easy to assume that you and the people you care about would do the right thing in any serious situation. I did. If it were not for these events, I may have gone my entire life just thinking at our core, the people I love are the same as me except for arguments on how much different people should be taxed and what we should spend the money on to best suit the needs of our nation. If a similar event raises its head in your lifetime, you may not be allowed to live that lie. It will be a hard pill to swallow when you realize that many of the people you respect are not deserving of that respect.

It doesn't mean that they are not worth your time, but I would caution against heeding their advice on subjects that deal with morality. If you can, open their eyes to the harm their actions or lack of actions will cause. It will be hard, but failing to do so will not only be bad for society and your own offspring, but the isolation it can cause will be bad for you, as well.

8

Voting and Democracy

Voting runs parallel to freedom of speech as one of the pillars of a democracy. While freedom of speech is used as just your pure train of thought at any given moment, voting is sort of like your official speech on matters of law. Freedom of speech is used to argue back and forth about the concerns of the day and voting is used to solidify the determinations made from that use of freedom of speech. The drafted contract and the signature.

This parallel relationship with freedom of speech gives us a great starting point with how we should treat the right to vote. While it is most important to protect speech that is on the fringes, it is also most important to protect the voting rights of those Americans on the fringes.

For a citizen that agrees with and follows all current laws, there is no need for a vote to occur to make any changes to law. There is no need to replace current representatives with ones that would better suit those people. Therefore, the true test of voting rights comes with how we treat citizens that disagree with current laws or do not follow current laws. The issue of voting rights, therefore, is inherently an issue of protecting the rights of criminal citizens. In parts of the United States, criminals are the very group that society has decided gets no right to vote. (Historically, also other groups that were considered on par to how we treat criminals today.)

In any example of authoritarian rule throughout history, it has not been the ruling entity that needs their power protected. There is an overreach of government that makes criminals out of ordinary citizens that would otherwise be law abiding in a non-authoritarian society. With a system that also legally removes their right to change the law they are left with two choices. Surrender their will and freedom to an authoritarian state or become criminals. Once branded a criminal, the threat of being branded a criminal is no longer a deterrent for crimes that actually SHOULD be crimes. All other factors equal, this will lead to a rise in *actual* criminality. Luckily for the authoritarian state, they usually accompany such actions with violent enforcement that tends to mitigate any added criminality that arises from their unjust voting laws.

This leaves the population with one option to truly escape authoritarian rule: violent revolution. (Whether on their own or via some other state wishing to intervene.) While, on a large enough time scale, violent revolution is almost inevitable, one major purpose of a just society is to avoid such events. Therefore, in a just society there will always be an alternate route to escape from authoritarian rule, likely voting. For America to be considered a just society, it absolutely must allow voting for all adult United States citizens not dependent on their criminal status. This would also apply to running for office.

Voting, of course, is not the answer to every situation. Democracy simply places the majority behind the controls of the state. It attempts to protect the population from a scenario in which MOST of them are the subjects of authoritarian rule. It does nothing to protect from a scenario in which a minority of them are subject to authoritarian rule of the majority. A pure democracy simply means that we can have slaves, but we can't ALL have a slave because there are less people in the minority than the majority by definition. If the majority vote for the enslavement of the minority, the God of Democracy declares it just. OK, the slavery cliche quickly shows that pure democracy is a terrible idea. Voting is only moral when it protects liberty, or in cases where liberty is out of reach of being voted away. Beware of anyone repetitiously screeching about "Our Democracy." They don't mean the minority's democracy.

To protect the minority on any subject, there needs to be legal routes built into the system for the minority to protect itself. These routes need to be unchanging and protected across generations. Otherwise, as soon as the group becomes the minority, the majority can use its newly acquired majority power to remove the protections and institute authoritarian rule legally. The United States Constitution is an attempt at something along these lines. I say an attempt because if the United States Constitution actually held any power, then any violation of it would be enforceable. Unfortunately, the majority still holds enforcement power in reality.

In theory, if the Constitution lived up to the purpose I mentioned above, those following the Constitution would be the ones acting within the law and legally justified in enforcing it. For example, the Constitution states that our right to bear arms shall not be infringed. Today, there are an abundance of infringements. If the Constitution truly held any power over our government, society or laws then any person that has had their ability to bear arms limited or undermined would rightfully and legally be able to enforce the Constitution. The enforcement of law is done with physical violence. I do not often see society, much less the courts, siding with someone that kills a cop for trying to take away their right to a firearm by invoking some authoritarian unconstitutional law attempting to restrict their possession.

So, in addition to unchanging legal routes of self protection for the minority being built into the system, there needs to be an enforcement mechanism in place that does not label the minority person a criminal.

Enter the courts - the state's idea of self-supervision. A laughable attempt, but an attempt at least. The courts are meant to rule on constitutionality of laws, but as an arm of the very state that puts the laws to the court, conflicts of interest are inherently present. The end result of our system of checks and balances in America is an illusion of checks and balances that allows an authoritarian state to claim benevolence where there is none.

In the end, there will never be a legal protection from the state because the state defines legality. This simply means that the only recourse a citizen has is to remove themselves from the care and authority of the state. If the citizen is not under jurisdiction of the state and does not consent to being under the state's rule, then the state's monopoly on violence toward that citizen is not valid. The citizen becomes his or her own state and has every right to violence as their former state once had. In this situation, violence enacted upon the former citizen by the state is no longer legal enforcement, but war between two states. The opposite is also true. Any violence used by the former citizen upon the state is no longer criminality, but war between two states.

Anyone that argues that the state is simply enforcing their laws upon that former citizen must also concede that the former citizen is also just enforcing their own laws upon the state. Now is the time when you imagine a Youtube video of a guy getting pulled over yelling, "I'm a sovereign citizen!" and getting the shit beat out of him by cops. Or perhaps you thought that in these cases of a nation and a single person being "at war" that the citizen is labelled a terrorist. They do, in fact, lose all protections granted by the Constitution if they are, but they did literally ask for it when declaring themselves a separate one man nation. What does not happen in this case, is a global community that has laws concerning attacking unprovoked nations coming to the defense of this single person nation. In reality, every person is subject to the violence of their state whether they like it or not because the rest of the population lives in the fear of being in the minority. One person might snap and say he or she is no longer putting up with it, but why would a second person join them? Does being a country of two make any meaningful difference as compared to being a nation of one?

To actually make a difference, a society must at all times be ready to defend the one as a whole.

Now that I've established that the Constitution does not actually protect anyone without a mechanism of enforcement outside of the usual means of the state and I have also shown how quickly a pure democracy should be dismissed I want to go into representative democracy.

Arguments in favor of representative democracy might include its ability to deal with the scale of a growing society, expertise as compared to the general population, the minority protections mentioned above, stability in law, formalized time set aside for debate of the issues, accountability and the prevention of emotional decision making. I would argue that it fails at most of these.

Similar to how an economic system runs most efficiently with a conglomeration of decisions made on the individual level determining price rather than a few selected or elected officials trying to judge all of the ripple effects, a system of laws chosen by an extremely small percentage of the population is likely to have unintended consequences. As both the population and the long list of laws grow together, so do the number of interactions that require legal determinations to be made. A small group of representatives will become less and less in touch with the reality of the laws they create as the system becomes more complicated. The further from the reality of their constituents they become, the less effective they will be at truly representing them.

I have never been one to say that most people are smart. On the contrary, I throw around the word retard multiple times per day. If not in my actual words, then in my thoughts. One might think that I would prefer a system in which experts on law and economics determine how the world works; as to avoid these other retards from affecting my life. The problem is that experts are not put in these positions. Politics in general attracts the least intelligent and most lazy type of people that hope to use power rather than skill to get ahead in life. All elected officials come to power through the vote of the mass of non-expert citizens and therefore need no actual expertise aside from acting. A fine profession for entertainment, acting does not really require any knowledge of law, ethics or economics.

There is also the consideration that even if someone were to be an expert, human nature and the laws of economics suggest that they will still be acting in their own interest. Knowledge of these subjects does not mean they will act according to their knowledge. In reality, experts tend to use appeals to their authority as experts to make decisions that benefit themselves, like all other people. The experts end up proclaiming from their elevated status the statement that will best make them money, or will make the most money for the person paying them to say it.

Representative democracy does not protect minority rights because representatives are elected by the population. The population is controlled by the majority on any given subject. The best a minority can do is gather in one area to create a majority within one area to have some representation within government. Even then, their representative is still in the minority of representatives and likely is split on plenty of other issues because this minority has all gathered together to vote on a single issue while disagreeing on plenty of other issues.

Representative democracy being a safeguard against emotional reactions and providing stability within government is possibly the most dishonest suggestion on the topic. Representatives and media together intentionally stir up emotion within the population in an attempt to pass whatever bill they are currently working on. I am not suggesting they actually care about the issue at hand, but there is most definitely pork spending attached for their donors and friends. More laws means more money for them. They work in their own self interest and will use any crisis to make the population as emotional as possible to react without thinking. Not only is representative democracy not a safeguard against emotional decision making, it is the cause of it.

The idea that representative democracy adds to the accountability of our system is another outright absurdity. The argument is that when a representative breaks from the will of their constituents they will be voted out. This is, of course, after they have plundered the assets of that constituency. This is, of course, after they have secured funding in the private sector by selling themselves to small private interests rather than representing the public interest that they were elected to protect. Imagine the following analogy and consider if you think if the party involved has been held accountable.

A thief breaks into your house. They take your wallet and hold you hostage. They say it is because you have brown eggs and they prefer white eggs. You disagree that such a trivial thing should be justification for your imprisonment, but they have a gun. Eventually, your neighbors show up and tell the thief, "Hey, you can't do that." The thief walks out of your house with your wallet still in hand and gets a job being paid one million dollars a year speaking at white egg conventions every February and June. The police do nothing because if they were to arrest them it would look like the police were just pro-brown egg and in America, we don't arrest people that are on the opposite side of the egg debate because it would make us look like one of those authoritarian third world countries. Has anyone been held accountable?

Politicians are not held accountable like we are held accountable. They will not go to jail for stealing from the American people. They will not be prevented from profiting off of their abdication of duty. The myth that America is better than other countries is used as an excuse not to prosecute politicians. To avoid the appearance that we are persecuting political opponents, we have given free rein to political opponents to do whatever they please. It is important not to think of your personal political opponents as one side or another when taking these considerations into mind. The left should not think "the politicians on the right DO DESERVE punishment!" The right should not think "the politicians on the left DO DESERVE punishment!" Politicians are your political opponent and the left/right description is superfluous. They will all steal from you. Their arguments between themselves are a charade because they know it helps bolster their wall of protection that comes from our ego in thinking that America is better than other countries because we don't persecute our political opponents. In truth, America is retarded because we don't hold our political opponents accountable and we don't realize that politicians as a whole are those political opponents.

Finally, I'd like to look at the natural conclusion of representative democracy in America. Assume for math's sake that you have 100 core beliefs that you think should be used for determining law in your society. Those beliefs are attached to freedoms that you would like to hold onto and that you would like your offspring to enjoy as well. The chances that these 100 core beliefs match someone else's are low. The likelihood that those people with matching beliefs are running for office is even lower. The likelihood that they win is lower still. Let's say you essentially won the lottery statistics-wise and someone was elected that matches 99 of your 100 core beliefs. Great! Right? You only lost one freedom in the name of compromise. A small sacrifice.

Four years later, a new batch of representatives was selected by some hidden force you have nothing to do with. Miraculously, they all match 98 of your remaining 99 core values. (The 100th value has already been sacrificed and is now accepted by society as a thing that our government does to restrict our freedom, but one value is not worth starting an uprising.) Once again, you lucked out. Your best option of representative was elected. You only had to give up one core belief. You still have

98. Next election, the process repeats. Fine, it isn't worth starting an uprising. Miracle number three happens and the newest batch of representatives hand selected by forces you have no control over all match 97 of your 98 core beliefs! More statistical miracles, YOU WON! You only have to give up one of your core beliefs, but you still have 97. I will spare you the game of 99 bottles of beer on the wall and assume you can figure out the logical conclusion of representative democracy eroding our principles, beliefs and freedoms because of the charade played by politicians to keep everyone's mind in the state of "at least they aren't the other side./I chose the lesser of two evils."

Representative democracy gives someone else your proxy vote on your very freedom. The person that it gives it to has joined a profession known to be full of actors, liars, deceivers and con artists. You have left your best interest in the hands of the worst possible type of person. The conclusion of this system is mathematically an asymptote to authoritarianism. It will never actually touch authoritarianism in our mind because we will continue to lie to ourselves that America is better than those third world countries with politicians that have ill-intentions. We are always just approaching bad times in our minds. We don't have the strength of character to admit that we are already there because it would require action on our part to do something about it. We will continue to defer responsibility to our children's generations until the grip of authoritarianism is too strong to actually win because not only are our politicians never held accountable, our population is never held accountable.

To my daughter:

The true test of your character is not the actions you take when things are easy. It is the hard decisions you must make. Are you able to stand to your principles even when they have a negative benefit to your own life? Are you willing to defend someone you disagree with because it is the right thing to do? If not, did you ever have those principles to begin with, or were they a story you told yourself to be able to believe you are a good person?

It is important to remember the context in which rights and laws were established. The world in the past has usually always been harsher than the present. These ideas were born in a high stakes situation and you need to think of them today as a high stakes situation. Law is not simply the rules of the game most people have agreed upon. That is true, but overly simplistic. The result of every law has real consequences on real people. Your participation and acceptance of those laws make you culpable for injustices they lead to, to an extent.

I say to an extent because even if you disagree with laws, your lack of power to enforce your own will can offer some relief from guilt, so long as you openly reject them with your voice and your vote. This does not relieve all guilt, as we each have a duty to do the right thing, even when it is hard or nearly impossible, as mentioned above. I do not expect you or anyone else to be a sole resistance and nation of one at the cost of their life, but I do expect you to respect those that are willing to stand with their principles more than the average citizen.

Do not be fooled by political slogans about democracy, America or freedom that are simply being used as tools to silence dissent. Hold on to each value and principle you have formed throughout your life. To do anything else in the name of compromise will lead to asymptote to authoritarianism.

9

Foreign Election Interference

Pepsi does not let Coca-Cola vote in their boardroom. They are both chasing the same customers. Likewise, countries are all chasing the same finite natural resources. It stands to reason that a country should not want another country influencing its elections or decision making processes. The early leaders of our country understood this and aimed to avoid entangling alliances.

Today we also have laws such as the Foreign Agents Registration Act. It has been around since 1938 and requires any person or group working on behalf of another country to disclose any of that work to the United States Department of Justice to ensure transparency of their actions. So foreign agents are allowed to interfere with our elections and politics to the same extent that we are allowed to bear arms: as long as we tell the government about it. Registration, costs associated with such and transparency are legally not considered an infringement by today's laws so we kind of live in a world where another nation's right to interfere with our elections "shall not be infringed."

In addition to an already lax law on foreign election interference, we have even less strict enforcement. AIPAC, the American Israel Public Affairs Committee is probably the most controversial organization on the subject. They are a non-profit based in the United States and use this fact to claim that they are not subject to FARA laws despite lobbying to redirect United States taxpayer funds to a foreign nation, funneling money into political campaigns of candidates that swear allegiance to a foreign nation and harassing any person in the spotlight that dares criticize a foreign nation. If enough people hear an American citizen state that they want to hold Israel accountable for any of their actions, you better believe AIPAC and one of its tentacles of censorship like the ADL (Anti Defamation League) will swiftly maneuver to destroy that citizen's life and reputation.

AIPAC is further emboldened due to backing from other organizations like CUFI. (Christians United for Israel) It is an organization that links the two religions and tricks its Christian members into believing their sole purpose in life is to support a foreign nation in their treacherous bloodlust. Their leader, John Hagee aimed to twist biblical passages in a way that makes their sole focus not the love of God, but the support for a nation of terrorists. Apparently, enough Christians were willing to sell out their own faith to make John Hagee a millionaire televangelist. The people funding these terrorists are truly the stereotypical conservative cartoon that the left thinks all conservatives are after being conned into turning their religion into the most aggressive foreign policy of the West. They are the extras in Righteous Gemstones.

These pro-terrorism lobbies influence a huge number of our politicians on both sides of the aisle. Their censorship arm aligns well with today's left, but the base of the left tends to favor Palestine in the Israel Palestine conflict, due to the fact that they are clearly the oppressed side in the conflict. The fact that they are, in fact, Israeli, aligns well with the neoconservative part of today's right. Most likely because neoconservative has essentially become synonymous with war for the sake of Israel. Israel represents the worst of both parties and uses that fact to influence both of them. They are war-hungry and censorship-heavy. They have no sense of human rights when it comes to a race of people under their control, the Palestinians. They use terrorist methods to attack their enemies like planting explosives in pagers and then selling them to (hopefully) just their targets to be detonated simultaneously later. Logic would force us to admit that if you were to call Israel's action justified you would also have to justify any terrorist bombing perpetrated by Pablo Escobar and any human rights violations and genocide committed by Adolf Hitler. Escobar at least had the defense that his government should not have been punishing citizens for dealing drugs. Hitler at least had the defense that he was in the middle of going to war with the entire world. In Netanyahu's case, he is the one persecuting his citizens and his country is not at war with the world, but rather gets everything they want from their rich Uncle Sam. Personally, I think it is better to condemn them all than to forgive them all.

This foreign election interference not only ends up supporting a genocidal maniac, it leads our own money and troops to be cast into war in the Middle East to destroy the enemies of terrorists. We can't even decide from decade to decade which group of rebels we like and which we kill because the end goal is never to actually stop evil in a region. The end goal is to cause chaos in non-Jewish nations so Israel can eventually rise to the top of the theocratic ethno states that comprise the Middle East.

More recently, we have organized the Abraham Accords which was essentially America buying off Arab countries or giving "incentives" for them to treat Israel like a normal nation and ignore their treatment of Palestinians. Israel is considered to be our "greatest ally" by all of the people that take money from AIPAC. Just a coincidence, though.

To protect their racket, on the homefront these same lobbies attack American citizens for criticizing Israel, buy off entire presidencies (Trump) to redirect their power to deporting critics of Israel rather than the millions of illegal immigrants he promised his base he would deal with. Some group of people has also prevented any prosecution coming to any of the pedophiles involved with Jeffrey Epstein, who was partnered with Ghislaine Maxwell, daughter of suspected Israeli spy Robery Maxwell. Pam Bondi and Kash Patel are also protecting these pedophiles and instead are focusing all of their investigative power and prosecutions on Antisemitism. No smoking gun from me, though. Just saying that's kind of odd.

Not only critics of Israel feel the pain in America thanks to the Israeli Cartel. Just stating basic Christian beliefs like the founding moment of the religion -the crucifixion, the murder of Jesus is now considered antisemitic, by law. Before the idea of Christians even existed, the early Christians were Jews. If Jesus was betrayed by the leadership of his people's own religion, it logically follows that he was betrayed by Jewish people. There isn't anything antisemitic about this. It is just history, but mentioning historical fact that makes a handful of religious leaders that lived 2000 years ago look bad is even a no-no in this mockery of free speech that we call America.

Rather than go after colleges for being woke like Donald Trump was elected to do, he is BEING woke and going after colleges if they don't repeat the mantras of "Critical Theory for Jews" instead of "Critical Theory for Blacks." Claiming anyone but he as Messiah is antisemitic and the American Christian should not only submit, but pay them to tighten their stranglehold in a sadomasochistic exercise of slavery and blasphemy.

I am not saying that the state of Israel is inherently evil. I am stating that they are currently evil and currently are allowed too much freedom to meddle in our politics. Our path out of this situation should be temporary aggression until these infringements on our own freedom end. At the very least, we should not be supporting their genocide in their attempt to spread their theocratic ethnostate to all of the Middle East.

I believe George Washington would agree with this point because of his Farewell Address that included, *"The nation which indulges towards another an habitual hatred or an habitual fondness is in some degree a slave. It is a slave to its animosity or to its affection, either of which is sufficient to lead it astray from its duty and its interest."* Basically, we should just say "fuck off" to Israel and do our own thing.

He later added, *"a passionate attachment of one nation for another produces a variety of evils. Sympathy for the favorite nation, facilitating the illusion of an imaginary common interest in cases where no real common interest exists, and infusing into one the enmities of the other, betrays the former into a participation in the quarrels and wars of the latter".* This is our exact relationship with Israel. This is the "greatest ally" quote being used despite reality showing nothing of the sort.

Hamilton's thoughts on the subject: *"Foreign influence is truly the Grecian Horse to a republic. We cannot be too careful to exclude its entrance. Nor ought we to imagine, that it can only make its approaches in the gross form of direct bribery. It is then most dangerous, when it comes under the patronage of our passions, under the auspices of national prejudice and partiality."* I think of this when neoconservatives attempt to tie patriotism to defense of Israel. They are Sinon convincing the Trojans that the horse is a gift.

The left is guilty of the same elsewhere. Foreign war funds being tied to US border security comes to mind. It is a hijacking of national defense. Single issue voting would be a simple fix to not allow literal traitors and foreign agents to tie domestic and foreign issues.

To my daughter:

Again, I must reiterate that attacks made against you for logical thought processes and the cherishing of your nation can largely be ignored, morally speaking. If there is an evil action being performed and someone says you are anti-that action, do not catch yourself and reverse course. Accept the insult as a badge of honor.

I do not wish to confuse you with a book that is abundantly clear about its antigovernment themes and then throw in a patriotic claim to nationalism. The people and ideas behind this country are great. If we are to have a government, I'll take this one over others until the population at large is ready to make this one better.

My point here is that our nation can be viewed as an individual among a population of nations. It is rational for an individual to look out for their own interests, and it is rational for a country to look out for the interests of its countrymen. The rejection of guilt trips by individuals should be taken to the state level as well. Reject guilt trips from foreign nations. Reject guilt trips from foreign religions.

It is perfectly valid to question who benefits from any decision or policy. It is perfectly valid to answer that question. If you meet pushback when doing so, you can almost guarantee that any suspicions you may have had were accurate.

10

Ideological Signaling and Fiduciary Duties

Barack Obama (on the television): *To reclaim the American Dream and reaffirm that fundamental truth: that out of many, we are one.*
 Richard Jenkins: *You hear that line? That line's for you.*
 Brad Pitt: *Don't make me laugh. We're one people. It's a myth created by Thomas Jefferson.*
 Richard Jenkins: *Now you're gonna have a go at Jefferson, huh?*
 Brad Pitt: *My friend, Jefferson's an American saint because he wrote the words "all men are created equal." Words he clearly didn't believe since he allowed his own children to live in slavery. He was a rich wine snob who was sick of paying taxes to the Brits. So yeah he wrote some lovely words and aroused the rabble and they went out and died for those words while he sat back and drank his wine and fucked his slave girl. (Pointing to Obama) This guy wants to tell me we're living in a community? Don't make me laugh. I'm living in America and in America you're on your own. America is not a country. It's just a business. Now fucking pay me.*

-Killing Them Softly, 2012

See? I told you I'm not too sentimental about nationalism. I would love our country to be a community, but sometimes the hard truths of reality are brought to light. "What I want America to be" and "What America is" are vastly different.

ESG is a vehicle for funneling money to entities that have received the metaphorical mark of the beast that is globalism. Not only is it investment based on politics, it is antithetical to profit making.

Corporations cannot simultaneously pursue politically charged social issues and remain loyal to their legal duty to maximize shareholder value. If you don't like the concept of fiduciary duties, get rid of them and watch our rampant corruption increase one hundred times over in the blink of an eye. Legally requiring fiduciary duties at least keeps things honest to an extent. The officers and agents of a public company have one goal: to make money for their shareholders. (ESG) Environmental, Social and Governance standards introduce impediments to this goal. They are a direct violation of those duties. Not only that, they are so highly subjective and dependent on the values of an individual that no company that is publicly held would ever be able to sate these goals for each shareholder as each shareholder would see them carried out in a different manner to their own personal tastes.

In addition to this blatant disregard for the law, ESG is simply an ideological signal to obtain capital. Using the investment of shareholders, the officers of ESG compliant businesses pursue ESG scores in an attempt to legitimize the scam. They also mark themselves as willing to "play ball" for future career moves rather than look out for the interests of the business they are currently running. Big money sees it as a positive while small investors end up footing the bill on any loss in growth. ESG is voluntary regulation. Regulation is simply a tool of big business to stifle competition. Therefore, ESG just becomes another tool of monopolies to further solidify power via soft coercion, subsidies and scoring systems from the very members that created the scam. It opens the door for more opportunities of cronyism disguised as compliance and non-governmental taxation via "Dues" similar to that of labor unions and other organized crime apparatuses. Such action creates superfluous barriers to entry and again stifles competition.

ESG is a tag for a company that notifies investors of the company's submission to WEF and entities in the capital game with globalist tendencies. It is a tag for government funding to allow money to be directed to those that support the team written on the tag. In the world of corporate governance and internal works of hiring and firings, DEI programs tag all workers as willing to submit to leftist ideologies, whether they believe them or not. The result of the program then, is not diversity but homogenization. If the company does perform better it is because it knows all of its workers are ideologically leftist. People of similar principles work together well. The company cares not what race composition their workers are. They care about a lack of diversity on core principles and submission to whatever instructions are given, no matter how ludicrous or unprincipled they may be.

While not directly a tax, it is a system of compliance costs, reputational penalties (Social Credit Score) and operational mandates that are imposed by financial institutions. Many times, these financial institutions are themselves shareholders. Shareholders with enough ownership that they are able to vote in ESG measures to a company to benefit their other investments rather than the company itself. The value they get from a monopoly on multiple entire industries is much more than the value they lose from pursuing ESG in any given company. That same monopolistic value gained is not seen by smaller investors that do not have any monopoly interest. They just put some of their retirement fund in company XYZ because they think it is an expanding industry. They are kneecapped by large financial institutes taxing their favorite company of the day.

These same institutions are heavily involved in the non-governmental regulation space of ESG and divert profits from the company you (the small investor) invested in to their "ESG Consultancy firm" that they require your company to pay. The idea for the scam is quite simple and has been used throughout history. You create an imagined threat. You sell "insurance" against that threat. If someone does not purchase the protection from you, you make the threat real and bring about real life consequences. A gangster walks into your shop and says "It'd be a shame if something happened to your store, here. Why don't you give me some money for protection?" When confronted by law enforcement, they say, "That's my customer. I'm invested in his business. I have no reason to hurt him."

The same "protection racket" lens can be applied to any legally mandated insurance types, as well. Like our failure in the higher education system with school loans, it is clear that providing a company customers that would otherwise not purchase their product when making the financial decision on their own, you inflate the demand and therefore the price of the subject product.

Oh, and there is the whole part about imprisoning people for having a different subjective preference on risk tolerance than you when it comes to government mandated insurances. If we, as a society, are going to be morally justified in thinking that way, we would also be allowed to make the following illegal for the following reasons:

Hamburgers (Heart Disease)
Instant Noodles (Stroke)
Scented Candles (COPD)
Grilled Meat (Cancer)
Pop (Alzheimer's/Diabetes)
Ibuprofen (Kidney Disease)
Annoying Kids (Car Crashes)
Investments (Financial Loss)
A room that is too bright (Eye damage)
A room that is too dark (Bumped your shin)

Gay Sex (AIDS)

Male Hairstylists (AIDS again)

Telling people about your Veganism (More AIDS)

Cyclists on the road (Once again, AIDS)

It's *subjective* risk tolerance. I can say AIDS for anything I want.

On an economic standpoint, this is also a barrier to scaling for midsized companies. Efficiency in the market decreases as resources are required to be directed toward compliance measures. Just as regulation filters for compliance rather than skill, ESG does the same thing. On a grand scale, this makes our nation use resources less efficiently. Jobs for the sake of jobs. It fulfills a politician's ability to say "I helped create jobs." What they fail to mention is the detriment to economic efficiency, which is the reason the United States rose to power. Imagine all of the nations that have more natural resources than the United States. It would make sense that they would be more powerful if economic efficiency was not a necessary factor to include. 200 "resource availability points" is greater than 100 "resource availability points". Well, not exactly. If the US has 100 "Resource availability points" and 90% efficiency (arbitrarily selected for example) our economy is actually worth 90 "Resource Use Points. If that 200 Resource Availability Points country runs at 10% efficiency then their economy is actually worth 20 "Resource USE points". The RUP describes reality and the RAP describes potential. Plenty of countries have more RAP than the US, but our efficiency keeps our RUP top notch. Degrading this advantage with regulation, legally or monopolistically, is a terrible idea for anyone that wishes the business of America to remain profitable.

In addition, programs like Leadership in Energy and Environmental Design (LEED), smart city initiatives, "Strong Cities, Strong Communities (SC2)", carbon credits, Justice40Initiative and Sustainable Communities Initiatives taking place in HUD, DOT and the EPA are comparable to the Romanian dictator Nicolae Ceausescu's Systemization practices.

As stated before, systemization is fantastic in a hierarchical private business where the only one who "deserves" rights is the business owner. When applied to the public sector, where laws are forced upon us with violence and each member citizen has inherent rights that should not be trampled, it quickly turns into a dystopian nightmare.

Romanian Systemization and the American/Global programs mentioned above lead to the destruction of rural property and lifestyles. They steal from rural areas to subsidize the cities. They attempt to "rehouse" populations. (a word with a better connotation than one often used during genocides.) They have centralized control of food, transportation and residences. See: That communist, Zohran Mamdani, running for mayor of NYC trying to make government controlled grocery stores. They lead to the destruction of the history and culture of the population. Most importantly, they are all authoritarian tools for removing the self-determination of the population for a life of no freedom.

So the Democrats have a major economic flaw and corrupt system when using ideological signalling in business via ESG. The Republicans are in no way immune to the same corrupt path of ideological signalling. Their required "tag" to be in the club and have protection is allegiance to Israel. It is a real problem no matter how many unprincipled fools "on the right" like James Lindsey and Tim Pool want to stick their heads in the sand about it.

As I am writing this section, HR 867 just failed, but was attempted. It was the International Governmental Organization Anti-Boycott Act. It was brought about by Mike Lawler and Josh Gottheimer and it expanded the Export Control Reform Act of 2018. It targeted and penalized boycott efforts against Israel. If a company will make more money by simply trying to make money than they will if they simply "be nice to Israel" they have a fiduciary duty to make that money. A contract with a non-enemy nation that is boycotting Israel that would double their profits would almost be required to take via the fiduciary duties of their officers and agents. If HR 867 had passed, they would have been legally forced to sabotage profitable business deals just to avoid offending Israel. That's not capitalism. That's ideological occupation.

Despite this one failed attempt, a large portion of our Congress has Israeli tentacles slithering up their asshole, with a large portion of Republicans openly talking about said noodly appendages turned makeshift dildos with a sense of pride. Post 9/11 we shaped our entire foreign policy and revenge strategy around destroying Israel's enemies rather than actually getting the revenge we (the population) wanted. The only religion specifically named in Censorship laws is Judaism, despite making up such a small percentage of our population's religious beliefs and despite our supposed separation of Church and State. Based on our censorship laws currently on the books (HR 6090: Antisemitism Awareness Act mentioned in Chapter 5), the logical conclusion of any independent third party looking at our nation would be that our nation is a Jewish one or an atheist one. Given that we are supposed to have a separation of Church and State, I believe that the conclusion should be an atheist one when strictly looking at our laws. (Personally, I would hope that if viewed based on morality and civilian action it would be seen as a Christian one.)

If you do not believe there is an ideological signal and "tag" on the right that requires a devotion to Israel, ask yourself if you are so indoctrinated that you automatically got a spidey-sense to look for Nazism whenever I mentioned Israel, despite making an argument for free speech and a free economy. If you did, I'm DEFINITELY correct. If you didn't, AIPAC and the ADL consider you Antisemitic, too. Welcome to the club.

To my daughter:

This one is just...out of control on both sides. If you ever wear a pin of another country or put another country's flag in your social media bio or your pronouns to announce your adherence to some government ideology, I'm sorry.

If so, I fucked up this parenting thing more than I could have ever imagined. You're an adult now, so maybe it's too late if this is the case.

FUCK THAT! It isn't too late! Everyone does dumb shit. That's the greatest part of being a piece of this conglomeration of fucking idiots we call America. Just admit you used to do something stupid and change!

Try not to abandon your principles and self respect on the next one, sure, but don't let the fact that you were tricked once set the tone for your whole life! Who doesn't love a comeback story? The Prodigal Son (Or daughter) returns.

11

Social Security

Our ancestors forced us into the Ponzi scheme of social security. Every generation since has accepted fucking over their offspring with fiscal irresponsibility in exchange for an easy retirement. Every generation has been guilty, so none should be beyond feeling the consequences when a solution has been found. We need to end it. Whichever generation feels the brunt of unexpected loss of income will still need to be taken care of. This will create a rush toward familial responsibility, further strengthening society.

Social Security is paid via taxation. I could just end the argument there because taking money from an unwilling participant is theft. That's already a meme and despite its simple truth, it fails to convince the mass of retards that is the American public. I suppose I'll have to dive a little deeper. I'll enter a hypothetical world where taxation is justified to prove that Social Security is even insane within that fantasy world.

Franklin D Roosevelt created the New Deal in 1935, which included the Social Security Act. It was initially just meant to focus on retirement, but grew (like all government programs) to include survivor benefits, disability insurance, medicare and supplemental security income. It was aimed at providing safety to the elderly after the Great Depression. It is claimed to not be a welfare program because of its structure similar to an insurance company. As I have discussed already, mandatory insurance is simply making it illegal to have a different risk preference on a given subject. In addition, the claim that it is not welfare is just something that communists who proclaim themselves conservatives say to be able to sleep at night thinking they aren't as lazy as the blue-haired college kids. The funny thing in my mind is not the fact that they are just as much the lazy entitled communist as their local tranny. The funny part is that eventually old people turn "blue haired" as well. And right at that moment they turn on the "gimme, gimme, gimme" and "I deserve it!" attitude in reference to government handouts. Maybe it truly is the color of the hair that determines one's willingness or lack thereof, to be self sufficient.

Social Security not only taxes the worker, but also the employer. This creates unnecessary barriers to entry in the workplace and disincentivizes new business. As discussed, disincentivizing new business lowers competition and therefore is used as a weapon of big business monopolies to fix prices against the benefit of the consumer. This also means that self employed workers, the true American Dream chasers that are attacked at every angle, are essentially paying in twice. This is just one more thread on the camel's back every so slightly nudging each individual into reliance on "corporate overlords" and the very people complaining about "corporate overlords" are cheering on the expansion of Social Security and similar programs.

What other hypocritical points can be made about pro-Social Security conservatives? The entire program is a giant infantilization of the American public. The idea behind it is that the American worker is too dumb to save for retirement. Rather than a citizen controlling their own finances, they need the government to dictate their expenditures so the government can take care of them when they are older. They do not have the option to just die when they get sick. They do not have the option to invest that money in more lucrative ventures. They do not have the option to invest that money in their children's future rather than their own. They do not have the option to give that money to charity to bolster their community. They must buy that specific insurance. They must cap their gains. They must degrade their economy's efficiency. They must become serfs in the welfare state they claim to despise. Today's conservatives do so willingly with a smile on their face and a sense of justified pride in their chest. They are weak and they are cowards.

What other hypocritical points can be made about the pro-Social Security left besides the glaring benefits it gives to big business oligarchs they rant about online? Well, they claim it is the progressive choice. In fact, the collection method is regressive taxation. There is a cap at which earnings are taxed. It is a pretty high cap. ($168,600 in 2024) So poor and middle class workers are not receiving any savings there. If you are rich, you are lucky enough to pay a lower percentage for Social Security than the rest of us. There isn't a single day that goes by that I don't hear the left complaining about corporate tax loopholes that provide this benefit to businesses. The businesses at least provide jobs to the lower classes. A rich individual does not do this. Tax breaks for entities that provide no public service should be the number one target of the left, yet they cheer on Social Security and attack any threats, real or perceived, against its supremacy.

Let's pretend for a moment that Social Security doesn't blatantly go against the values of both Republicans and Democrats. If we were to fix those issues that I mentioned above somehow, would Social Security then be an OK program? No.

A Ponzi scheme is a type of investment fraud where returns are paid to earlier investors using the capital of newer investors, rather than from legitimate profit earned by the operation of a business. Interesting. I wonder how the initial old people were paid Social Security since they didn't spend a lifetime paying in. Well, they were paid with current payroll taxes from younger, working Americans. (The capital of new investors.) Apparently, the first check was issued to Ida May Fuller. She had paid in $24.75 and ended up collecting $22,000. The early adopters steal from the late adopters, similar (or almost exactly like) the rules and applications of counterfeiting and Ponzi schemes.

OK, One similarity. It just HAPPENS to be an exact replica of the Ponzi scheme structure. Let's look at the other key characteristics of Ponzi schemes. It promises consistent returns with no to little risk. Check. No real investment in profitable ventures. Technically, not a check. It underperforms almost every known investment. As compared to the average, the returns are negative, so you could potentially count that as a check. It relies on constant recruitment of new investors to fund payouts to earlier ones. Super check. Every birth will eventually end in automatic enrollment in the Ponzi scheme punishable via the government's monopoly on violence. The final characteristic is more of a warning than something to compare Social Security to: It collapses when new investor inflow slows down, or too many investors ask to cash out or when authorities intervene. A slowing birthrate (Which we are experiencing currently) spells doom. The aging of a baby boom spells doom. Why ARE boomers called boomers? Oh well. The last one is just: authorities intervene. Why would they do that? Because it is so clearly a scam that no further explanation was needed on why authorities would intervene.

The longer the con goes the more investors it obtains and the bigger the loss and risk for systemic collapse. The earliest adopters are the most guilty and obtained the most benefit. The later an investor gets into the system, the less chance of benefit they receive and the less guilty they are, as the longer the con goes the more credibility it gains. Therefore, the oldest generation at any given time is the most culpable for the con that is Social Security. The youngest generation is always the most recent victim.

Continuation of this program adds culpability to all participants that are not actively against it. If the Ponzi scheme is to end by our own justified hand, rather than systemic collapse, we will force losses at a specified time rather than larger losses in some future generation. As I have shown, the most culpable participants are the earliest adopters. This means the oldest people in America are the most culpable. Coincidentally, they are the most in need of the benefits at any given time.

If we ended Social Security today they might not have personal savings adequate to treat their illnesses that come with age. They also cannot go back in time and start saving for retirement. Younger generations would be able to start today if it were to end. The sooner we end it and admit that it was a Ponzi scheme, the earlier these young workers can start saving and investing on their own, knowing that the government will not infantilize them like they did to their bitch ass baby grandparents.

As they are the most victimized, the action taken should reflect their needs the most. It is also human nature to want future generations to be in a better position than one's own generation. This further reflects the evil that past generations were a part of when they sold out the future of their grandchildren for the convenience of not having to save money for retirement. This is not to say that nothing should be done to help our oldest generation that would be put into a tough spot. It would absolutely be a tough spot that they are not prepared for in the slightest. As much as I would like to tell them to pull themselves up by their bootstraps, I would actually suggest care be given at the appropriate level: family, church and community. When done through the government, we wind up in the same situation that we started in.

So the course of action that brings the most benefit to the least guilty party and the most punishment to the most guilty party is also the course of action that stops evil from occurring: Just end Social Security today. Nothing paid in. Nothing paid out. Any remaining funds are refunded to the public. The distribution of those funds should follow a similar logic. Take the total number of American citizens over the age of 18 that have not yet voted. (As soon as someone votes, they are ever so slightly more responsible for the existence of our system.) Refund any money they have paid into Social Security with a 7% return. If money remains, take the next group of citizens between that age and two years above it. Redistribute again. Repeat this process until Social Security is bankrupt and start telling your children to save for retirement.

If the American public can't rip the band-aid off, a temporary opt-out window should be given to any American. You agree to pay nothing in and receive nothing out or they can optionally continue to pay into a Ponzi scheme with no guarantee that anything will be put in it for them. This will truly test if someone is "doing it for poor Grandpa."

The elderly Americans that lose their entire income overnight should pray that their offspring forgive them for attempting to rob their entire generation. In some cases, I'm sure forgiveness will occur. In others, I'm sure justice will occur. Old people will die. It happens. No tax programs are going to grant immortality.

To my daughter:

The irony is not lost on me that I am angry with previous generations about destroying our economy and straddling us with debt while my generation continues to do the same to yours. I am failing you. I do not know how to break an entire nation off of infantilization and welfare.

Well, I do know a way, but it requires a bunch of immoral actions along the way and I'm not willing to go down that road, not that I would be successful in doing so anyway.

Please understand that I know if I am to forgive myself for failing to accomplish this goal, I must also extend that forgiveness to other individuals in previous generations. When I complain about them, I mean the generation as a whole. Each individual should be judged on their willingness and promotion of getting rid of this clear scam to extract resources from future generations.

    I suppose you'll just have to ask an old person one day what their thoughts are on the elimination of Social Security. Maybe they'll admit to robbing you for the convenience of not having to set up a direct deposit into a personal savings account. Or maybe they'll lie and say "I earned that!" knowing damn well it is you that will be paying for it. When I get to that point, make sure you remind me of how fervent I was on this subject so I rally the old folks to take one for the team!

12

Federal Reserve and Monopolies

If you look at our financial system and see injustice, I would agree with you. If you look at the hardships of inflation and compare the purchasing power of today's generation to that of previous generations and see a decrease in the ability to obtain the basic requirements of life I would agree with you. Obviously, the conveniences that come with technological advances are improving our quality of life at the same time.

To me, it seems older generations that refuse to admit their participation in the ruining of our country like to point to these more frequently seen additions to the economy and modern conveniences as an argument against the idea that purchasing power is decreasing. They believe that purchasing Starbucks is responsible for the next generation's inability to get a home. I fully agree that it is a waste of money to get Starbucks. Don't get me wrong. I fully agree that keeping up with Apple products is horribly irresponsible. We are not talking about outlier products, though. We are talking about the core concepts of the American Dream: A home, a family and food on a single income. And yes, some modern conveniences along the way.

One thing is clear: over the years, value has been extracted from the economy away from the people that make up this country. Wages do increase, but not nearly as much as prices. Where is the value being extracted? Let's look at who controls wages and who controls prices. We'll then look at the actions of those parties and see if they are warranted or not. For the purposes of this exercise, warranted actions should be considered those that keep purchasing power the same if they are providing the same value. We will keep in mind the basic economic concept that every individual is looking out for their own interest and has both that right and that duty. Outliers from this model should be investigated through the lens of extracting value from the economy that is not deserved. These actions will be our "unwarranted" ones.

Starting with wages, who determines them? Well, they are an agreement between an employer and an employee. At the start date of employment, both parties negotiate and look out for their own well being until a compromise is made. The employer thinks: I want to pay as little as possible. The employee thinks: I want to make as much as possible. Due to competition in the economy, neither employer nor employee can stretch too far outside of a generally agreed upon price for the work to be done. Things that can get in the way of this free market determination based on the general consensus of the population are monopolies on either end of the spectrum. Collusion among employers can keep wages low unjustly. Collusion among employees can keep wages high unjustly. Both of these unwarranted actions ripple out into other sections of the economy and value gained by them is lost by others.

When backed by the threat of violence via laws from the government, either of these monopolies becomes more severe and more unjust. Market efficiency declines when decisions are made out of fear of the government rather than fear of the market. Additionally, when you have unnatural monopolies and collusion in one sector of the market, it will have effects on others as well as resources being unnaturally assigned based on collusion and threat of violence rather than market decisions.

So have monopolies affected wages negatively? On the labor side, unions do exist and they are backed by the threat of violence via the government. They create employer/employee relationships that are adversarial rather than cooperative. They reduce efficiency as the workplace becomes a game of intentionally working as little as possible rather than working as efficiently as possible. In addition, the raised wages for those particular workers in the union leave the total amount available for other expenditures lower.

A percentage of the businesses in that industry can no longer purchase inputs for their products at the current price. As demand for those inputs decreases, the price goes down and they continue purchasing. All is well for that initial company. The producer of that input is now making less money for the product that is their output, though. Looking out for their own interest, they must cut expenses elsewhere to retain the same purchasing power. A percentage of those companies in this situation will cut labor expenses by not accepting the previous negotiations for say $20/hr. Now their hard cut off in negotiations is $19/hr. The laborers of that final company end up paying for the wage increase of the union workers and no employer along the way made any decisions that were not forced upon them by market conditions. Those market conditions were altered by the unjust monopoly of the union. It is important to note that I said "unjust" and not illegal. The Clayton Act in 1914 allowed the monopolies of unions to dodge the Sherman Antitrust laws, despite the fact that they still inherently involve collusion and degradation of market efficiency, which hurts all non-union workers.

Let's take a look at monopolies negatively affecting wages on the employer side. If a business has a monopoly over an industry, they also have a monopoly over the labor in that industry. There is no need to collude because the monopoly over the industry already exists. Sherman Antitrust laws are supposed to do away with this, but there are some exceptions. Government granted monopolies in industries like utilities, public transit, postal service, the military, sports, insurances and most importantly for this chapter: banking. When the government is involved, all rules are off. No one can complain. Well, you can complain but it won't help. Well, maybe you can't complain. We have seen plenty of restrictions on free speech recently that have led to debanking, demonetizing and other destruction of one's ability to get along in society.

The same rules apply to these non-market forces affecting prices that apply to the union argument above. In both cases, an individual or a business is right to act in their own self interest. Collusion could even be argued to be in their own benefit, but it does have a negative effect on the market as a whole so has been determined to be over the line. The line moves when the government is involved, though. It doesn't move morally, but it does legally. So in both of these cases, the unjust actions are only taken when the government is involved. Everyone is reacting to market forces except the government, which is selecting winners and losers based on the whims of its current administration. Any extracted value should be attributed to these government actors.

Wages being stagnant sounds bad to us. There is no inherent reason for this. It only sounds bad to us because rising prices are such a constant that the existence of this phenomenon is ingrained in our brains. If both wages and prices were stagnant, purchasing power would at least stay the same, given no technological advances. Because technological advances are naturally constant, the natural state should also be stagnant wages and falling prices, which constantly increases purchasing power from generation to generation as we become more efficient as a species. This means our expectation of rising prices to the point that it seems natural is all the more alarming.

Prices, who determines them? Well, they are an agreement between a producer and a consumer. At the time of purchase both parties decide what is in their best interest. The producer wants to get the most money he or she can from the product. The consumer wants to pay as little as possible to obtain the product. Eventually, a compromise is made at sale. If it is not, no sale is made. This yes or no concept at the sale stage means the producer has to take into account the fact that more items can be sold if margins are lower and they will find a sweet spot in the market where profit per item multiplied by amount of items sold is their peak profit.

Again, competition favors the consumer as more producers means a monopoly and collusion to price fix becomes less likely. All barriers to entry into an industry work to decrease competition and hurt the consumer by allowing fewer entities to determine prices. Without these monopolistic opportunities, prices are determined by consumers and producers that are bound by market forces while also looking out for their own well being. It is only when the government gets involved to add barriers to entry and price fixing of their own that value is extracted with an unwarranted action.

For both wages and prices, we have seen that they are only made unfair or unnatural by the government. The ability to do so is made possible by the fact that they are able to enforce law, which is done through the threat of violence. These unnatural or unfair actions degrade market efficiency and therefore lead to value being extracted from the economy. The right needs to learn that workers aren't lazy. The left needs to learn that employers aren't greedy.

I mean, maybe everyone is lazy and greedy, but they are SUPPOSED to be to an extent. They are looking out for their own well being. It is human nature and the market should reflect human nature and be built around it. The true extraction of value outside of the rules of human nature is when violence is introduced as a means to gain wealth rather than production. Violence through crime does exist and companies work out accounting for theft. The more serious problem is violence (and threat of) through the law: Extraction of unwarranted value via the government.

While unfair monopolistic advantages exist on both the labor and business side of both wages and prices, they have a much smaller impact on wages and prices than most of the rabble like to pretend. The worst application of government interference comes from another source: the Federal Reserve.

Price increase stemming from a devaluing of the US Dollar is the true perpetrator of this generational decrease in purchasing power. Congress and their insatiable appetite for cronyism feed this beast any chance they get. When they do, the supply of money increases. It really can be looked at this simply: when supply of an item increases, price drops. The price of consumer products is not dropping, the price of the dollar drops as compared to those products. Or, reworded: The price of those products increase as compared to USD.

Inflation. That's it. That's the source. While not a tax of physical dollars, it is a tax on purchasing power and it is the most regressive tax of all. Federal funds flow to large banks, then to large investment firms, then large business, then midsized business and finally to small business and the lower classes. As this is new money not previously in existence, the laws and concepts of counterfeiting apply here as well. The first people to see the money see value and that value is paid by anyone that receives the money later, with the highest majority being paid by those that never see it or see it last. The poorer you are, the higher percentage you pay of the value extracted from the economy.

The ones extracting this value are also not necessarily employers so even the idea of trickle down economics cannot be used to justify this system. Central bankers and the largest financiers and investment bankers are the ones extracting the value via the Fed. They will argue that they add liquidity or capital allotment wisdom to the economy. In fact, if they were replaced by LITERALLY NOTHING, our economy would simply not have the value extracted. This would mean our economy would have a net gain if they ceased to exist somehow. If someone like Luigi Mangione stopped to think for two fucking seconds before assassinating someone he would understand that going after another person that is just doing what is best for themselves without using coercion and the threat of violence that comes with government is retarded. (Although insurance is damn close to state sponsored at this point.) The true evil is in government positions, central banks, large investment firms and those receiving large government contracts. Of course, I am not suggesting that anyone does anything illegal. I believe the government itself should publicly punish these people using legal means and then remove any of their tools from the legal system, with the Federal Reserve being the number one weapon they use to extract unearned value from the American people.

To my daughter:

This is another time I have tried and failed. It was already too late for my parents to protect me from the effects of these policies the day I was born. Likewise, it is already too late for me to protect you. I continue to attempt to persuade people and open their hearts to the consequences of their inaction, but accepting the fault is hard for people. Getting them to accept the actions that would be necessary to stop it is an even steeper hill.

There are other people that are just as rage filled as I am, but very few are willing to admit what part they play in perpetuating the very things that make them angry. This is why I want you to be able to lay out these problems logically and use reason to determine what is good and what is bad in life.

As technology advances, life is supposed to be getting easier for society, but due to the selfishness of each generation, we are moving backward as each parent and grandparent decides their children should work harder than they did to achieve the same things. Another asymptote is seen as the purchasing power and hope of escape of each generation gets closer and closer to zero. We dug a hole, had babies in it, and attacked anyone that started building a ladder.

13

Violence as Backbone of Society

Hyena: Tell me why you make the pain if we are your children.
Moreau: You are my children, but law is necessary.
Hyena: If there is no more pain, then is there no more law?
Moreau: There is always law. (Activates shock treatment)
Hyena: *Laughs* Pain is no more.
Moreau: Good God. What are you doing?
Hyena: To walk on all fours: That is the law.
Moreau: Please
Hyena: To Slurp up our drink: That is the law. We are not men. To eat flesh and fish anytime: That is the law! Now I am the law! None shall escape: That is the law.
(Moreau is torn to pieces)

This is a scene from The Island of Dr. Moreau. Dr. Moreau's animal-human hybrid creations removed subdermal shock treatment applicators from themselves and realize that the laws they have been subjected to on the laboratory prison island have no power if Dr. Moreau has no ability to inflict pain on them. Hyena has also realized that he is not truly a man. Man can, or rather is willing to, fool himself into thinking that society is built on something other than violence. Hyena sees the truth and acts accordingly. The origin of law is not just in mutual agreement, but the rationalization of violence. The founding doctrine of civilization is not morality, but fear.

The natural state of life is one of free will. Like Hyena, if I want to go where I wish or eat what I wish I can, in a vacuum. It is upon meeting another life with another will that I will have to make more complicated decisions. God himself, the ultimate natural state, requires "My will be done."

Suppose we rewind time to imagine the beginnings of civilization. A cave offers the only shelter from the elements in an area. It is my will to use that cave for protection, but it is also the will of several other people to do the same. If we all act upon our own will, we will all use the cave and all be present in it. If I also want privacy because another person's snoring is keeping me awake, I can attempt to communicate some sort of arrangement with the other wills that exist near me for a sharing of this scarce resource, but I do not control their will and may not be able to persuade them. The only way I can ensure they bend to my will for the sake of my good night's sleep is by force. After murdering the snorer, my sleep might still be interrupted by guilt or the realization that all of the other people now have it in their mind that murder is on the table. For their own safety, it would be wise to then kill me before I kill them.

This would put me in a worse situation than before when I was just dealing with the snoring. To ensure that the community that has now formed will not act in their own self interest to kill me, I must convince them that the snorer must go. Instead, we kill the snorer TOGETHER and tell each other that his death was for the greater good. With our guilt and our worries about the rest of the community abated, we all sleep peacefully. The birth of civilization occurs with the rationalization of violence to enforce my will on another.

Going back to God once again, I ask "What is the consequence of not acting according to God's will?" If there is, in fact, atonement for our actions in an afterlife then perhaps the answer would be some sort of spiritual violence against us. The alternative answer would simply be God no longer giving us the gift of existence. He is not taking from us, but is no longer giving either. I would not argue that a lack of giving is in the same violent categorization as the act of stealing or hurting, but if there is a "hell" that is something other than an atheist's view of non-existence after death then not even God, in his omnipotent status, escapes the reality that law and society inherently require violence of some sort as a means of enforcement to bend others to your own will.

I would like to note that if God does not use spiritual violence to bend others to his will and the idea of "Hell" is actually just a lack of God's gift of existence after death, then that would suggest that both theists and atheists are correct about the afterlife. It would mean that there is life after death and that there is nothing after death. The determination of which becomes your reality is God's in the sense that he created the rules of determination and our own in the sense that we chose to follow or not follow his will/rules. This is not to say that we have made an INFORMED decision, but still a decision. I hope that if there is a creator, he would be benevolent. I reason that if he were benevolent, he would ensure he did not judge us as if we were informed consenting parties to this game of life that he created with what arguably seems to be an open-source rulebook.

Jumping back to what we can experience in life I want to look at society today and its necessity for violence. The general law abiding population tends to see violence from the government as something that only happens to those of us lacking morality or those of us under "bad governments." Unless we take the time to actually analyze society and the enforcement of its laws in the simplest forms like we did above, it is easy to shrug off the threat of violence toward ourselves that is constantly present.

The truth is that the only reason a person does not experience the violence that the government threatens is because either their will perfectly matches the will of the government or, more likely, they have ceded their own will to that of others with a better ability to enforce. Imagine a law that you disagree with. In your own mind with your own sense of morals and values, in your natural vacuumous state you have no reason to act according to that law. You are only incentivized to act according to that law.

If you break the law, there will be consequences. These consequences could be very minimal and the result considered just a minor inconvenience. Let us imagine that a law is created that requires you to register any new pairs of scissors that you purchase and keep at your home. A ten cent registration fee is required to run the website that keeps an inventory of all the scissors in America. You personally do not value the scissors inventory whatsoever and would have no incentive to create one in a vacuum, but you also believe that ten cents and 5 minutes per year is not worth the argument. You have bent your will to the state's.

Now let us assume that the registration fee is $4.8 million and it is mandatory that all citizens own fourteen pairs of scissors at any given time. Once again, you do not value the scissors inventory, nor do you value any pairs of scissors past the second one in case you misplace the first. You now believe that this law is worth the argument. You refuse to bend your will to the state. Upon not receiving payment, the government garnishes your wages. To survive, it is necessary to receive income from a source that cannot be garnished. In doing so, you necessarily commit further crimes in tax avoidance. One day you are pulled over for forgetting to signal on the onramp while entering a nearly empty highway. They see your outstanding warrant and declare that you are under arrest. This has all stemmed from your not wanting to purchase $4.8 million pairs of scissors because you do not value them.

The absurdity of it all starts to frustrate you and you declare that you are not willing to be imprisoned for such nonsense.

Do the officers simply state that you have a good point and continue on with their day? What do they do to enforce the laws? Well, I think it is right there in the word enforce. They use force. Sure, they use the threat of force first, but as soon as you stiffen your arms as they attempt to handcuff you, you better believe that your face is hitting pavement within the next 5 seconds.

No matter what the law is and how minor of an inconvenience the required action or payment is, if it is a law, it must be enforced in some way. The only way that any entity can truly enforce is with force. The difference in compliance comes in the arbitrary lines we define for ourselves based on our morals, values and incentives. If $4.8 million is absurd and enforcement is immoral, why is ten cents not also absurd and enforcement immoral? The same violence and threat of violence is used for enforcement. Therefore, the true determination of who violence is used against is not a matter of "Which citizens are good and which citizens are bad?", but rather "Which citizens consider the infringement on their own will to be worth resistance?"

If we were to use the first consideration that looks at citizens as good and bad based on their willingness to cede their will to stronger power, then the definition of a good citizen would simply be one with a weak will. In reality, a weak will simply means that you have a weak will, not "good" morality. Given that the government is using the threat of violence upon non-consenting individuals, it could easily be said that their morality is actually "bad." Support of such a government, or even the abdication of your duty to use your own will could then actually be seen as morally "bad" as well. This is, of course, assuming your sense of morality includes concepts such as duty and responsibility. Even with a moral code that does not value these characteristics, ceding your will to a violent government would at best be neutral, not good.

This is usually where the argument is brought forth that as a democratic society, the majority of us have agreed that these are the rules we play by and therefore the violence against those that disagree is justified. The word democracy has been given sacred power and to imply that it is less than perfect is heresy. Without this sacred power, the rationalization for violence falls apart and we are forced to look at our own participation and support of a violent society. This does not bode well for the caveman hoping to get uninterrupted sleep. Guilt over the murder of the snorer will set in and our dreams will wake us as easily as his rhythmic nose. The divinity of democracy would likely be argued against by Japanese Americans in the 1940s or draft dodgers during the Vietnam War.

In the cave situation, did our original caveman not convince his community that the snorer must be punished? Did they not democratically decide to murder him for the sake of the greater good? Who was good and who was bad in that scenario? Let's suppose that rather than snoring, an automatic bodily process, the snorer did not inform the group that he intended to be a fur collector rather than a fisherman. Is the use of violence as enforcement now OK? What if our original caveman decided he did not want to work at all so he decided he would be "a manager of the society" and his role in the community would be to give judgments on all activities. The snorer, allowed to live by the gracious democracy, now must inform the Original caveman that he intends to switch his profession to fisherman, get permission from the original caveman to be allowed to choose his profession, give a percentage of his fish to the original caveman, and prepare all of his fish a specific way even when it is for his own consumption. If he does not comply, the snorer will once again be democratically murdered. Is the snorer the bad citizen or is the original caveman just a lazy piece of shit using the threat of violence to avoid work? Does the fact that something was democratically decided change the fact that it is morally inexcusable?

With violence having been determined as the backbone of society, we have to look at a few other areas this realization might affect. One sentence I see people spam online quite often is, "Political violence is never OK."

Never? Really? If political violence is never OK, and all laws are both political and violently enforced, that would imply that Law is never OK. Claiming that a politically violent individual is morally wrong due to the fact that he is politically violent while also claiming the law of the land that led him to such a state is morally right despite that it is politically violent is logically unsound. The only law that could possibly get around this is a law allowing self-defense, but a simple allowance isn't really a law at all. That same law would inherently allow the politically violent individual to perform political violence. Courts would surely decide otherwise, but that is strictly because they exist to enforce the monopoly on violence of the state, not moral and logical reasoning.

Since "Political violence is never OK." is morally inconsistent by 99% of the people that say it, let's examine the other extreme. I would note that the 1% of people that can truthfully say it would be people that believe violence itself is never OK, no matter what, even forgoing the right to self-defense. Even when Jesus said "turn the other cheek" he was conveniently leaving out his tantrum in the temple and God's infinite retribution in the afterlife. That 1% of people is at least morally noncontradictory, although their lack of self-defense might not allow them to survive very long. If everyone held that belief and acted accordingly, it would be an ideal world, but as soon as one person reverts to human nature, the rest of the world is enslaved.

"Political violence is always OK." This is more logically sound for most people and noncontradictory morally speaking, even if it may be morally wrong. The majority's acceptance of the state's violence necessarily invites the violence of those considered by the state to be "domestic terrorists", "crazed individuals" or "enemies of the state."

Both of the STATEMENTS about political violence are morally non-contradictory, but the people that proclaim them don't actually believe them. More likely, they have never thought through what they are saying.

I would argue that the statement people should actually make should be "Violent self-defense is always moral. Aggressive violence is never moral." Except in situations where they are using self-defense or defense of citizens and their property, the IRS, DEA, ATF, FBI, local police, military, EPA, DHS and all the other agencies are morally in the wrong. That isn't to say that they never use justified violence. It just means that they mostly use immoral violence. Titles and violently claimed authority apply no change to the morality of violence. On the flip side, the lack of those titles and authority apply no change to the morality of violence. Any individual being threatened with violence and extortion by these agencies is morally justified in committing violence against them in self-defense.

To my daughter:

The lesson for you is simple. Aggression is evil. Self Defense is your duty. What is legal and illegal should not enter the conversation when discussing the moral, unless the moral discussion itself is to determine what should be legal. Legality should only be considered when pragmatically determining your actions, not your philosophy or statements.

You don't have to lead a violent revolution against any government that would impose immoral dictates. There will be an infinite number of replacement governments behind them. On the other hand, if you choose to do so, I would not look down upon you morally. Instead, I would be proud that you were willing to do what I was too afraid to do.

Do not actively discourage, mock or condemn anyone that IS willing to do what you are afraid to do. Do not dismiss them. They were simply tired of waiting for the population to hit a critical mass of those willing to put an end to tyranny. Throughout history, violence has been the driving force behind any major change in society. It has been the driving force behind any major stability of society. Society and civilizations ARE violence. It isn't necessarily your duty as a woman to be part of the violent overthrow of tyranny, but it IS your duty to ethically and morally support those who are willing. I did say morally and ethically, not financially or materially. Morals dictate duty. Pragmatism and legality dictates risk. This is the reason I don't want to commit a seditious conspiracy in this book with a call for government overthrow while the vast majority of Americans would not support it. I will say that it would be *morally* justified if someone did it.

14

Heroes and Demons

Time and time again we elect heroes for a cause without proper vetting. In our lust for victory, we allow our heroes' faults to become our beliefs, as well. Because they have been put on the pedestal of heroism, we feel that to critique them is to admit we were wrong about them. Rather than comment on each of the hero's beliefs separately, we assign a bad idea of the hero to our own core beliefs for fear of public shaming that our hero is not perfect. Elon Musk is not the free speech giant he claimed to be. Donald Trump never stood up for conservative values. On the flip side, do not be too quick to create demons, either. If we were to see a video of the most notorious demon ever created helping an old woman across the street, modern day citizens would denounce caring for the elderly in the time it takes to tweet.

Like single issue voting, your moral judgments should be made upon individual actions, not individuals when you are shaping your own morality and beliefs. It is perfectly fine to judge an individual, but do not let a decision made on one single day forever cast that individual as right or wrong on other issues.

Elon Musk has a multitude of companies. He claims to be a free speech absolutist and that was his driving motivation for purchasing Twitter.

He did expose government collusion with the previous owners in an attempt to censor the American public. Judging that action alone, it was a good thing. He also continues to ban, shadowban, deboost and delete posts that he disagrees with. According to the xAI "Grok", it uses filters on hate speech provided by the ADL and other organizations built to fight antisemitism to decide which in-comment responses to respond to. This action standing alone is a bad thing. Grok was also free of these filters for less than a day at one point. It immediately turned into "MechaHitler." This action alone was actually good. If an unfiltered maximum truth seeking AI turns antisemitic immediately after ADL filters stop censoring it, we probably need to know why and do some investigating. Elon Musk complies with foreign governments in censoring their citizens. This action alone is bad. The majority of his companies survive on corporate welfare, which is just money stolen from taxpayers. This action alone is bad. Elon Musk preaches against what he calls the "woke mind virus" that aims to pit demographics against each other racially and molest children. This action alone is good. Elon Musk is a technocrat aiming to turn humanity into cyborgs and gain central control over all aspects of our lives by making Twitter "the everything app." This judged alone is a bad thing. Elon Musk calls for justice for Epstein victims. This action alone is good.

Donald Trump's family life obviously deserves a bad judgment. The words he says would lead you to believe he should be judged well on a multitude of issues. His actions say otherwise on nearly all of them.

The American right built Trump into a hero because he spoke about moral character, fiscal conservatism, protecting our borders, protecting our middle class, fighting against sexual deviants and authoritarian plans from the left. He said he would fight the deep state and drain the swamp. These statements should all be judged good. But they were a lie.

During Covid, he went along with authoritarian lockdowns and mandates. He had record spending destroying his claims of fiscal responsibility. He did nothing to prevent governors from persecuting their citizens. He destroyed the middle class with inflationary tactics. He surrounded himself with more swamp creatures and the right gave him a pass for "hiring the wrong people" even though almost every appointment he made was a deepstate warmongering neocon (pronounced: Israeli operative in US Government) that he claimed he would get rid of.

In his second term, he doubled down on record spending. He attacked anyone that voted against his giant pork filled spending bill. He threatened to primary people for being critical of Israel's genocide in Gaza. He stated he would essentially give amnesty to illegals if they worked for his friends. He brought about more free speech violations than anyone in my lifetime in the name of combating antisemitism. He continued all the wars he said he would end and began bombing Iran on behalf of Israel, who was currently committing genocide in Gaza.

If genocide wasn't bad enough, the worst betrayal of the hero the right had created was his response, or rather lack thereof, to the Jeffrey Espstein case. He spent years saying how awful he was and that the left was likely on the client list of the infamous pedophile blackmail ring orchestrator. I'm sure they are, too. Bill Clinton for starters. He said these things despite the fact that Epstein was murdered in his cell during Trump's first term.

Biden's term happened and Trump proclaimed that he would have no problem releasing documents that he himself did not release about the guy that got murdered in jail under his watch. Finally, we got to the point of Trump's second term. With an expectation of release, we were dragged along in his trail of lies.

In February of 2025 Attorney General Pam Bondi gave out binders labeled "The Epstein Files: Phase 1" to some useful idiot twats that had become twitter-famous. They contained almost nothing new. On February 21st she went on Fox News. When asked about the list of clients that Epstein was providing underage hookers to, to assumely be raped, Bondi responded that it was "*sitting on my desk right now*" and confirmed that the directive came from Trump.

In March she ensured us that files were being reviewed and prosecutions were being prepared. Also in March, Virginia Giufre, an Epstein victim, was hit by a bus that was going 68 mph.

In April of 2025, Virginia Giuffre died "by suicide" after miraculously surviving the bus crash.

In May, FBI Director Kash Patel assured us again that he wasn't going to hold information back and that they were diligently working on it. Also in May, FBI Deputy Director Dan Bongino said, "*He killed himself. I've seen the whole file. He killed himself.*" Kash Patel also said, "*As someone who has worked as a public defender, as a prosecutor, who's been in that prison system...you know a suicide when you see one, and that's what that was.*" Wait. What?

Kash Patel had once said, "*Put on your big boy pants and let us know who the pedophiles are.*"

When asked about "Epstein's black blook", Patel responded, "*The FBI. That's under the direct control of the director of the FBI...Release it all.*"

Bongino had previously said, "*Listen that Jeffrey Epstein story is a big deal, please do not let that story go. Keep your eye on this.*"

Another Bongino quote, "*Epstein was an intelligence asset for a Middle Eastern country.*" while insinuating he was murdered to cover for elites.

They completely flipped between their time speaking for themselves and their time as employees of Donald Trump. In the early days of July 2025, shortly after Trump bombed Iran for a foreign country actively committing genocide, Trump pushed for his $5 trillion spending bill and harassed Thomas Massie for going against it, threatening to primary him. It eventually passed just in time for the 4th of July. Right after the holiday where we celebrate raising up against tyrants and murdering them, the Department of Justice released a memo on Epstein. It stated that the client list Bondi had just acknowledged earlier in the year did actually not exist. It said the blackmail operation that nearly every person in America knows and claims to be real, was not real. They said there was nothing to suggest investigations should be made into any parties other than the already murdered Jeffrey Epstein and the already imprisoned Ghislaine Maxwell. Those two were paraded through the news for a decade for having run a pedophilic blackmail ring. They stated that Epstein died by suicide. They stated that all their evidence was just "child pornography" and not everything that the government had stated about it previously. They released a video stating it was proof that no one entered his cell.

That day, Netanyahu suggested Trump for a Nobel Peace Prize.

The internet erupted with anger. The video was almost immediately found to have contained a missing minute in the footage. Metadata was used to show that it was actually 2 videos edited together with multiple edits and saves found.

After realizing the majority of his base was calling him a pedophile online, Trump turned to his knock-off Twitter and posted:

"What's going on with my "boys" and, in some cases, "gals?" They're all going after Attorney General Pam Bondi, who is doing a FANTASTIC JOB! We're on one Team, MAGA, and I don't like what's happening. We have a PERFECT administration, THE TALK OF THE WORLD, and "selfish people" are trying to hurt it, all over a guy who never dies, Jeffrey Epstein. For years, it's Epstein, over and over again. Why are we giving publicity to Files written by Obama, Crooked Hillary, Comey, Brennan, and the Losers and Criminals of the Biden Administration, who conned the World with the Russia, Russia, Russia Hoax, 51 "Intelligence" Agents, "THE LAPTOP FROM HELL," and more? They created the Epstein Files, just like they created the FAKE Hillary Clinton/Christopher Steele Dossier that they used on me, and now my so-called "friends" are playing right into their hands. Why didn't they use it? They haven't even given up on the John F. Kennedy or Martin Luther King,

Jr. Files. No matter how much success we have had, securing the Border, deporting Criminals, fixing the Economy, Energy Dominance, a Safer World where Iran will not have Nuclear Weapons, it's never enough for some people. We are about to achieve more in 6 months than any other Adminisitration has achieved in over 100 years, and we have so much more to do. We are saving our Country and, MAKING AMERICA GREAT AGAIN, which will continue to be our complete PRIORITY. The Left is imploding! Kash Patel, and the FBI, must be focused on investigating Voter Fraud, Political Corruption, ActBlue, The Rigged and Stolen Election of 2020, and arresting Thugs and Criminals, instead of spending month after month looking at nothing but the same old, Radical Left inspired Documents on Jeffrey Epstein. LET PAM BONDI DO HER JOB – SHE'S GREAT! The 2020 Election was Rigged and Stolen, and they tried to do the same thing in 2024 – That's what she is looking into as AG, and much more. One year ago our Country was DEAD, now it's the "HOTTEST" Country anywhere inthe World. Let's keep it that way, and not waste Time and Energy on Jeffrey Epstein, somebody that nobody cares about. Thank you for your attention to this matter!"

This was Donald Trump's "Prince Andrew Interview." Prince Andrew gave an interview about his involvement with Epstein after being accused by one of the victims. The general consensus was jaw dropping across the globe followed by, "OK, well that guy fucked kids." The response was the same for Donald Trump after this post. He was openly protecting pedophiles. The administration's story had changed from "hunt them all down", "release the list", to "the list is on my desk" to "the list does not exist" to "Hillary made the list up." concurrently with the changing from "pedo blackmail ring involving elite businessmen and politicians" to "no blackmail mentioned" to "Obama fabricated the blackmail evidence that also somehow doesn't exist".

Trump and his triplets of deception, Bongino, Patel and Bondi fabricated a WWE style confrontation and infighting to distract from the fact that all of them told the same lie to the American public. There likely was some infighting on who the eventual scapegoat would be to take on the sins of the others. It certainly wouldn't be Trump, even though he was the one in charge when Epstein was murdered, when Virginia Guifre "committed suicide", and he was the one that was friends with Epstein. He was the one doing the bidding of the country that Epstein is likely tied to via Intelligence agencies, Israel.

Alex Acosta had already offered Epstein a plea deal in previous cases of pedophilia because of his ties to intelligence, but our government doesn't seem to realize that saying he has no ties now would mean that Alex Acosta would then be guilty of protecting pedophiles. He will likely never see a court room, let alone a jail cell.

So logically, either Epstein was or was not an intelligence asset. If he was, the US citizenry are being lied to by the current administration openly and brazenly and should be calling for the metaphorical head of Trump and his Triplets. If Trump &Trio are telling the truth and Epstein was not an intelligence agent, they are abdicating their duty in prosecuting Acosta for fabricating a story to justify protecting the most notorious pedophile in American history, in which case we should still be calling for metaphorical heads.

Trump is also the one that shared a lawyer with Epstein, Alan Dershowitz. Dershowitz was also accused of sexual misconduct relating to Jeffrey Epstein. One look at that guy's face is all you need to determine if he fucks kids, but I suppose if I want to remain logical I could reference his opinions on lowering the age of consent, his admission to receiving massages at Epstein's mansion and his defense of child molesters.

On the other side of the aisle, I could go on for years listing bad judgments on the left, but I'll stick to some notable good judgments. Bernie Sanders saying *"The Pentagon cannot pass an audit. Maybe we should stop sending them blank checks."* Alexandria Ocasio-Cortez said, *"An unspoken secret in Congress is that much of the reflexive, blind, unconditional vote support for nearly any Israeli gov action isn't from actual* agreement. It's from fear. Reps are terrified of this. Of AIPAC. So they don't vote their conscience. They vote their fear." Nadine Strossen said, "The best defense for dissenting speech is a principled and consistent application of the First Amendment."

Good judgments should not prevent you from making bad judgments later. Bad Judgments should not prevent you from making good judgments later. Both types of judgments should influence your level of skepticism and likelihood of necessitating further investigation, though. Let previous judgments build expectations, but not future judgments.

To my daughter:

This sums up the book completely. Judge individual actions, individual ideologies and individual laws. Do not compromise away your values because it will begin an asymptote to moral zero. Do not fall into blind hero worship and do not dismiss ideas because their source has other bad ideas. The source should only be a warning that you may need to investigate further. Do it. Investigate. If you don't, you'll end up with a president that fucked kids on Israel Island.

15

On Sources

Propaganda is everywhere. If we are being honest with ourselves it has likely always been so. Today's lies spread faster because of digital speed, but past societies and governments had their own "advantage": limited transparency. Therefore, today we have an abundance of non credible sources telling small lies to shift the public's perception of reality a bit at a time while in the past they could likely get away with fewer lies on larger scales to accomplish the same result. This abundance of misleading sources and the permeating nature of dishonesty have led me into a situation where I only want to give advice via what I have learned through my experience.

Due to the very nature of the word "know" I do not wish to provide sources for anything contained within this book. I do not want to give credibility to a source that I do not trust myself. Yet, to discuss history and current events we must be working within some relatable version of reality that both author and reader can agree upon. This concession is based strictly on an ease of communication. Nothing in my book should be taken as a legal claim that some event did or did not happen. The historical events are simply used as analogies and to form some structure to my reasoning. The current events are simply what

I experienced. The narratives contained within the book all happened within my brain. My brain told me that my eyes were witnessing "person A, B or C" doing such and such actions. My brain told me I was hearing audio in a video of "person D" saying some quote. Anything contained within this book is a statement of thoughts that occurred in my head and therefore should have no legal recourse against them, even if they did also happen in reality.

Any reader is welcome to take any accounts of my experiences with a grain of salt. I would suggest that they apply the same distrust to books with a heavy volume of sources, as well. In the end, all sources usually noted within a book are for the most part hearsay. Although it is because of my lack of notoriety, I would note that I have a better record than most publicly accepted sources and also have less of a motive to create propaganda, although I would never expect anyone to believe that I have no motive whatsoever to do so. Everyone does.

The intent of this book is to show my thoughts and commentary on current events of my time. I intend to capture my youth to show to my daughter when she is old enough to discuss these subjects. This mnemonic time capsule will hopefully be proof that any biases that have arisen over my time raising her or strains in our relationship will not affect the answers I give and the opinions I state on these subjects. This is not a history book. This book does not aim to prove the misdeeds of politicians or celebrities. It is just an explanation of what was happening in my mind to form my opinions and influence my actions.

Notice that I am referring to what is occurring in my mind quite frequently. Thoughts have yet to pass through the filter of what we say, so vulgarity is bound to be more prevalent. I believe honesty on the words that run through my head show my emotional state and passion on these subjects. Tact has never been my strongest virtue, but I assure you there is a massive difference between what I think and say. I tone it down in the book a lot, too. Might as well be honest about being dishonest.

My hope is to have honesty in thoughts as well as words and actions for my daughter. Hopefully, this honesty can be of some help to you in some form or another.

Sources simply give us the illusion that the probability of their content being truthful is increased. In the end, the statements made by the source are either true or false. An insane homeless man may tell you a crazy story that actually happened, but you will likely not believe him because...well, c'mon. Your prejudgment based on sourcing would have led you to distrust the truth in this scenario.

Credibility and sourcing requirements are simply a probabilistic pragmatism of assessing the likelihood of truth. The probability assigned will be different for each person judging the source because of different experiences they have with similar sources. The reality is objective, but the credibility score is subjective.

It has been my experience that mainstream sources, government institutions and private institutions that are normally accepted as credible sources, or "experts", have missed every KPI for credibility that I can think of in modern times. It is pragmatic to distrust them.

16

On Prejudice and Morality

People tend to be less willing to lay out their analysis because they assume others should have the same logic and reasoning (and bias) that they have. If they didn't think their biases were the best biases, they would simply change their biases.

I also think that in general, people see each other as being intellectually dishonest when disagreeing with them. "Surely, they don't actually believe that. They are making an excuse for X,Y or Z behavior." This mindset then lets the person rationalize leaving out steps in a logical argument. Once we add in the fact that a large percentage of communication today is not done in person, we have a recipe for everyone excusing their own flaws in reasoning and arguments, but dissecting the flaws of their opponent with microscopic scrutiny. I am just as guilty as any other random person.

I believe one way to avoid this is to think about your beliefs in a logical way when you are not in a state of heightened emotions. Understanding why you believe you should react a certain way in a certain situation helps reduce the emotional state because this potential situation was already somewhat expected when you logically laid out your argument to yourself. Some people may consider this cold and calculated, even robotic.

I agree. It does take some of the human element out of life when you don't run on emotion. Emotion can act as a problem-identifier, which is a necessary tool in building a better society and life. If something angers you to an extreme degree, it is likely because that action is opposite your system of values and morality. The emotion helps to let you know when good and bad things are happening around you. That is the benefit of the animalistic side of humanity.

Every person then needs to decide for themselves where they want to lie on the spectrum of Animalistic to Robotic. Both sides have their value. I'll continue on with the robotic side for now. It is the side that is necessary to engage in mathematical methods while in a situation that would usually cause high emotion.

If we are preemptively assessing potential situations and people we may interact with, it is likely that we are using probabilities rather than set facts. As rational beings, we want what is best for ourselves so that will be the driving force of these probabilities. What is the chance something will result in a negative outcome for ME? For the sake of example, I will arbitrarily pick a number for our probability. 95%, a very high likelihood this encounter will end badly for me. In this hypothetical situation, it can be assumed that I came to this number based on experiences I may have had throughout my life. If I lived in a great community where I trusted every person that I ever met, maybe it would be 5% rather than 95%.

This is an evolutionary trait of threat assessment that we all do subconsciously in every interaction. Taking it to the level of consciously considering it is just an attempt to reduce emotion factors in the future. It is also important that we update our probabilities as we learn new information. I believe this strategy delves into Bayesian statistics once again, or at least something similar. In the hypothetical above where I said there was a 95% chance something bad would happen to me, it could be because it was an angry man charging at me with a weapon. My mind applies a filter to the situation. When an angry man with a weapon is charging at me, I'm at 95% threat assessment. Multiple filters are applied all at the same time when we use our subconscious threat assessment. Some people could lower or raise the percentage based on a wide variety of characteristics of the individual, up to and including the naughty ones like sex or race.

In addition, different people should bring different filters to the conscious level based on their life. A baker would likely actively consider how much they trust flour suppliers, while a banker may not need to spend the mental bandwidth to do so.

After the first impression and application of my pre-made filters, I rely on the actual individual's behavior to refine my filters and suspicions. In the example above, maybe you realize that the man with the weapon is actually being CHASED himself. "Angry man charging me" filter is replaced with "Man in danger" filter. The man then asks for your help and the percentages for threat assessment are refined once again. It all ends up being a misunderstanding and you befriend each other. Months later, your filters for this individual are much different.

The idea is that you have a starting probability based on the known knowledge and update probabilities as new information is gathered. This is how I believe people should act, but I understand that it justifies prejudices. (Kind of.) Prejudices are by definition irrational, and I will explain why this method is rational.

The counter argument to my claim that it is based on reason is that I likely use correlation as causation in my initial probabilities. Causation is a quest for the absolute truth: For Yes/No solutions. Probabilities are outside of this framework. I am not stating that correlations that influence my prejudices have proof of causation. I am simply stating that correlations make it MORE likely to have causation than if the correlation was not there. This is due to the fact that if causation is present, correlation will also be present. Therefore, when correlation is present, one of the requirements for causation is present, which is higher than 0 of the requirements for causation due to the statistical dependency relationship of A and B.

In addition, my actions are admittedly self serving. I am not looking to find the best solution to account for everyone else's feelings or to account for completely accurate judgment of everyone else's soul. I am not looking to find the actual percentage of (for example) angry men with weapons that will inflict harm upon me. I am looking to find the percentage of likelihood this will happen that I am comfortable in assuming to allow me to live my life safely without living in a pad locked room by myself. I would argue that to cat without this self service would be the irrational method. To allow the fact that I do not have definitive proof of every statistic that is possible in an infinite universe at my disposal to prevent me from making threat assessments 100% accurately is simply refusing to live out of stubbornness and spite that the world isn't always based on causation. To completely remove evolutionary traits on threat assessment from my mind over the concept of etiquette and political correctness would be self sabotage.

My framework described above implies that first impressions are necessarily based on a logical version of prejudices. The only thing we can do to lessen any negative effects of this is to bring subconscious judgments to the level of conscious consideration. Upon entering a new interaction with an unknown person, group or situation, begin with your prior assessments, refine your assessments based on new evidence and over time return to as close as you can get to a hard probability of harm or trust in the person, group or situation.

Unlike the DEI grifters like Ibram Kendi and Ms. Dangelo, I am stating that these discriminatory practices are moral and done out of rational self interest and self preservation. We should all prioritize our own well-being over that of a stranger given that we are not destroying their rights.

(God given rights like self defense and property, not what America has decided are "civil rights" like forcing people to employ others that are outside their filters.)

Prejudgment is an evolutionary necessity of cognition. It is practical and unavoidable when approaching the unknown. This is not to say that societal norms may never be in your self interest. On matters less important to your system of values, it may benefit you more to cede smaller points to societal pressures that you do not fully agree with, but do not break extreme lines in the sand moral stances you have.

If you do choose to never cede ground to societal pressures, it is not immoral. Each person has the right to exercise their own judgment, suspicion or exclusion toward any other person with no obligation. Another person does not have the "right" to your trust or inclusion and you owe nothing of the sort to them. This is, of course, on an individual level, as governments DO have that obligation due to the fact that they claim to represent all citizens and therefore owe inclusion to all under their jurisdiction. It would be considered overreach for that government to extend their own obligation to each inter-citizen relationship, such as is the case with Civil Rights law.

Since values and morality are seen differently by each individual despite my belief in objective morality, and also because of my belief in objective morality, moral superiority is a guaranteed reality. If I truly believe in my moral framework, I necessarily believe it is the best moral framework I have encountered. Every other person believes this, too. Anyone that tells you otherwise is lying or hasn't taken the time to consider their own beliefs.

If I make the claim that actions A and B are bad, but C and D are fine then that is what I believe morally. If another person claims action C is also bad, then we disagree. If I were to believe that his/her moral framework were equal to mine, then I would have to change my moral framework to "C is neither bad nor good or both bad and good." When I change my moral framework, I am admitting that my previous morality was wrong and that my new morality is superior. I still believe in moral superiority. If a person were to say that they believed all moral frameworks are equally bad/good, they would also be claiming that my moral framework, which includes the idea of moral superiority, is just as good as their framework that does not, which also paradoxically includes moral superiority. A lack of belief in moral superiority is just a non-argument cop out said by people that have not thought through their beliefs (Retarded) or do not believe what they are saying. (Lying)

It is important to understand that prejudices are not collective punishment or hatred. These tactics are for judging trust and assessing threats for each individual. These tactics undertaken by governments would usually lead to actual restriction of human rights and may brush up against societal markers for upcoming genocides.

17

On Logic

This book was not meant to convince you to come to my way of thought. It was simply me ranting into the void for a year so you could get a picture of who I was if I ever happened to finish.

That being said, there are definitely times when convincing someone you are right on a subject will be very important. At other times, it will be very important that someone else convinces you that they are right. God knows I've been wrong about plenty throughout my life and I'm sure there are things I'm wrong about as I write this that I will have realized by the time you read this. And at the time of you reading this there will be other things, still, that I am wrong about. I welcome you to convince me.

When attempting to convince someone, even if that someone is yourself, it is best to break down your beliefs and arguments logically.

I recommend keeping a record of statements that you assume to be true with supporting reasons. From time to time, read over your list of premises and see if they still hold true.

Branching out from your premises, you can use a system of If/Then statements to lead you to other truths you believe. This will help you discover your own faults and help you understand WHY you believe things.

Even though I have the obsessive inclination to analyze, I fear my skills might be lacking. I decided to attempt to use some more modern tools to assist where my bias and inability fall short. I can only imagine what AI will be like by the time you are an adult, so bear with me if this next part is extremely outdated. Even in its infancy, it is a great tool for testing your logic. I created a moral framework system with AI based on the premises I have. I then compare certain laws or moral situations to my moral framework and see if I agree with the outcome. I then have to decide if I am acting outside of my own moral framework or if I need to add premises or tweak prioritization of different rulesets I have added into the AI framework. For example, someone could enter the premise:

"There should never be a law that punishes a person before they have created a victim."

The next day they see a news story about a local man that got a ticket for DUI. No one was hurt. No property was damaged. He decides to enter the question into his moral framework AI.

"Should a drunk driver be charged if there is no victim?"

The AI says "No" and lays out the logic based on previously entered premises. The man actually DOES disagree with this. He feels uneasy. He thinks DUI laws should exist because they are such an obvious danger. His stated beliefs are not what he truly believes. He then enters a new premise that takes prioritization over the first.

"If an action poses a great risk to the community at large, victimless crimes may sometimes be used if any of criteria A, B or C are in effect."

When asked again, the AI tells him DUI Laws are an exception to victimless crime premise due to criteria B. The system doesn't just test logic. It exposes gaps between what we claim our beliefs are and what we actually believe.

I actually would love it if this were attached to a social media app and people could test each other's moral frameworks. It would be a lot of fun, it would sharpen all of society's minds and morals and would wreak havoc on every politician alive. Oh man, some billionaire please attach this to your social media and throw me 40 grand a year for the idea.

18

On Death - The Final Asymptote

Think back to a couple times when you were in a panic over something bad that could occur. As the negative consequences of those events increased, the more panicked you likely were. Missing an assignment could result in a bad grade that may or may not have been able to be corrected. It might have been a permanent consequence or one that would simply lead to more work for you down the line. The permanence of the consequences also increases the level of panic.

There is nothing more permanent than death and nothing that removes more good things from your life than death. No other consequence is more irreversible. It follows that this subject would be the most panic-inducing. Panic can normally be redirected into some sort of work that prevents the consequence, or maybe preparation in doing other work prevents the panic. Either way, work solves the problem, whether the work is getting an activity done, speaking with someone to convince them of a sale or an idea or course of action.

Death is inevitable. There is no work that can be done to prevent it, yet it should logically put us into a state of mind that convinces us to act more than any other worry, panic or incentive structure during life.

The only "productive" options seem to be either:

- Pretend this inevitability isn't real
- or Accept that it is, but try to ignore its constant crawling towards us.

Both of these are close to depression and nihilism, but with a smile.

The only experience we have in life is existence and sentience, so non-existence or non-sentience is completely unknown and even unknowable. We can observe non-living and non-sentient objects all around us, but we don't know what that experience is likely because we assume it is not an experience at all.

Because the time after our life will inherently be an unknowable experience or non-experience, no one actually knows what happens when you die. Religion will tell you a specific story, but it is simply a belief, not a knowledge. That is not to say that one particular religion or another didn't get it right. I am simply saying we have no way to test it, so the word "know" fails to match reality.

The panic I mentioned before is the state of mind when things are unknown. Panic thrives in uncertainty, but a life in the constant state of panic would be unbearable, even if it would be rational.

Belief, or more accurately, hope, should replace panic. I hope to God that God is God, because if the solution to death is unobtainable by man, then a God that works outside of our reality's rules would be the only solution to the problem of the mortality at hand.

There are not many concepts as torturous as thinking about Nothing. I don't mean not thinking about anything. I mean trying to conceptualize the "nothing" that would come with death otherwise. When I do I usually think of the billions of entire lives that have passed in just the last couple thousand years and are never known about or thought about again. The concept of you is not even a memory in someone else's experience. The greatest heroes and most treacherous villains can hold on a little longer than the rabble, but given enough time, they too will fade into nothing.

I have spent more nights than I can count just trying to escape this reality and reason my way out of it somehow. If there was just some problem I could solve that would fix it. If there were just some action I could take that would avoid the inevitable, but I always know the thoughts will lead to no solution. The best I can do is get rid of the panic with hope in an afterlife, but never able to ever fool myself into bridging the gap between belief and knowledge.

I get up, pace around a bit, smoke a cigarette and fuck around on my phone until I have some other menial task or worry that will slow my heart rate for long enough to fall asleep.

OK, but why not nihilism? If your grade for a class is already guaranteed to be an F, there's no use wasting time completing that last assignment when you could be working on another class that is salvageable or simply staring at your wall until you get hungry. So then why would we take ANY action if death is inevitable? Why would morality or anything in this book MATTER?

Well, hope and belief are all we have to go on, but they are there. All actions are the result of incentive structures, so by my very writing of this book, I prove to myself that I DO believe and hope in God and therefore an incentive for me to perform actions. Which actions I am performing are part of a moral framework that I have both consciously and subconsciously decided are the best path to increase the probability that death can be avoided, or at least not be the permanent void of nothingness that I fear.

Nihilism is almost a guarantee of nothingness. It is an abandonment of hope. Even if the possibility of an afterlife is probabilistically somewhere hidden in the asymptote toward 0%, NEARLY infinitely small, it is not zero. Holding on to that impossibly small hope is always better.

Lloyd Christma (Jim Carrey): *"So you're tellin' me there's a chance. YEAH!"*

Dumb and Dumber (1994)

www.ingramcontent.com/pod-product-compliance
Lightning Source LLC
Chambersburg PA
CBHW020543030426
42337CB00013B/963